THE
SYSTEM

THE
SYSTEM

What We Can Learn When Science and Reason Collide with Scottish Football

Graeme McDowall

First published by Pitch Publishing, 2023

Pitch Publishing
9 Donnington Park,
85 Birdham Road,
Chichester,
West Sussex,
PO20 7AJ
www.pitchpublishing.co.uk
info@pitchpublishing.co.uk

A CIP catalogue record is available for this book
from the British Library.

ISBN 978 1 80150 089 0

Typesetting and origination by Pitch Publishing
Printed and bound in Great Britain by TJ Books, Padstow

Contents

*This book is dedicated to my wife Gillian,
my son Aiden and daughter Carla, and
to my parents James and Celia – and to
all the kids who love to play football!*

A vision for Scottish football

SCOTLAND AS a nation that regularly produces top-quality footballers, players who typically start out playing in Scotland. A country where our best club teams regularly make it through the group stages of European competitions and can compete in the later stages. The clubs below our top teams are also a hotbed of talented and technical players, ready and able to take a step up.

Our top players often move to bigger European leagues, to the big clubs, and when they do they attract significant transfer fees. When they move on, they're replaced with younger, but equally good, and sometimes better replacements.

Our top league is highly competitive. Such is the quality and quantity of good players that the league winners are randomly distributed between the top four or five clubs, and occasionally a team outside of this will run close.

Our national team regularly punches above its weight, our technical style of play is a match for anyone. We not only qualify for European and world finals, but we also play in them with optimism and with a confidence in ourselves. It's a stage our players deserve; they enhance tournaments, they showcase their technical ability and showcase the success story that Scotland has become for producing top-class footballers and really good football teams.

Lastly, but most importantly, it's a game that children love to play and through which they can express themselves and develop the character and qualities needed to enjoy a good life!

Preface

LET ME begin the book by making my position clear. If Kenny Dalglish, Jimmy Johnstone, Denis Law, Billy Bremner, Jim Baxter, Alex James or any other Scottish footballing great had been born 300 years ago you would have never heard of them, because at that point football hadn't been invented and there would have been no outlet for their future greatness. Likewise, and for similar reasons, if they had been born 30 years ago, you probably would never have heard of them either. To this extent, it's my belief that in the last 30 years hundreds of players of the like mentioned have been born in Scotland and subsequently lost to the nation because of 'The System' of the 21st century.

For those great players who would become household names and legends of the game, the system of the 20th century allowed their greatness to flower and be shared. This means that there are players waiting on us to sort The System out, to allow them to share their greatness in the same way – and that's the task in front of us. It's in developing the outlet that allows for the expression of this potential before this generation or subsequent ones are also lost to the game – that's what's at stake here!

In many ways the book is a collection of the type of discussions, debates and arguments I've had in staff rooms, at dinner tables and while standing on the training field – and all in the context of football and how we get good at it. The likes of:

- What links the past with the future?
- What is talent? How would you define it?
- Are the processes of talent identification, selection and development fit for purpose?
- Do we over-coach young players?
- We should have won the 1974 World Cup!
- What age should children get serious about the game?
- Do we have too many or too few pro-youth players?
- Why do we have the elite system we have today?
- Did Scotland really invent the passing game?
- If you gave a bunch of kids a ball and an open space, why wouldn't they ask for some cones to set up a training drill?
- If you want to make better predictions, pay more attention to the Ls. Those who are sometimes <u>Late</u>, can <u>Look</u> a bit <u>Lazy</u>, a <u>Little</u> over weight and are <u>Lacking</u> a bit of physicality. Random factors out of their control often govern these things!
- Why we need to close the first-team pathway!
- A team from the central belt of Scotland, made up of Scottish players, could compete in La Liga!
- Have you ever fallen on a red ash pitch? If not, why not?
- Why Scotland should have at least one more professional club!
- How old is a 14-year-old?
- Why are Brazil not Brazil any more?
- Who was Scotland's last world-class player?

People who know me will recognise these ramblings and could probably add a few dozen more, and there's more in the book. They're captured and organised in such a way as to add some evidence to the arguments. To try to flesh them out in in a reasoned manner, drawing on science, anecdote and experience. They're set out in such a way that people can pick holes in the argument and show me the limitations of my own thinking and knowledge – hopefully this will stimulate and encourage further and more productive discussions. I don't need to be right, but I would like us to get this right!

About the book

THE BOOK tells the story of *The System* for player development in Scotland, and does so by looking at the past, the present and the future. It's a story inspired by what appears 'today' to be a system that's broken in its ability to consistently produce footballers who enhance our teams – both at club and national team level!

When it comes to the football aspect of the book, I don't claim to have any unique access to Scottish football. I'm an outsider in every sense. That, however, may be an advantage I have, as with any problem there can be a 'curse of knowledge' for those closest to the issues. In this sense outsiders have an advantage over insiders because they're less rooted and defensive of existing viewpoints.

The biggest motivation for writing the book is that I feel it's a game that's misunderstood when it comes to young people and their involvement and progression within it. When it comes to the 'science and reason' part, it's not a scientific piece of work. It merely draws from the scientific literature in an attempt to share my interpretation of what's known and how this applies to the system of today and what the future one might look like. It's hoped that on reading this book there's something for everyone in it.

Many people will be familiar with several of the discussions, but others won't be! It will hopefully be a useful piece of work to provoke reflection but also further debate and understanding.

This book is also not written from within the formal pro-youth system (or System 1 as it's referred to throughout the book). I didn't request or seek access to those currently working in the system. Nor did I seek to interview the perceived winners or losers among those who lived in System 1 for years. As such, I didn't interview the parents of kids who might tell a story of how harshly their child was treated, the opportunities they did or didn't get, how the coaches had their favourites, how their child was played out of position or suffered for any other reasons. As such, there's limited references to these voices, and where there is, they're largely anecdotal and should be treated as such.

Likewise, I didn't seek the viewpoints of the winners: those who stayed the course and reached the holy grail of a career at a high level in the game. In both respects this would only have been a distraction. This isn't a story of winners and losers. When it comes to how we 'fix' Scottish football, everyone has an opinion on this – academics, journalists, podcasters, members of the public, past and present players, coaches, this book and everyone in between. Perhaps the only thing everyone would agree on is that we need to do better, and that the status quo isn't an option!

The first section looks at Scottish football from a historical perspective. There's an important distinction to make here. A historical account it is not – that would be a book in itself and there are many good ones to already choose from. The historical context detailed is for the perspective it can give us about the present, and in such a way that can help to sharpen our vision of the future. A necessary first step to arrive at the conclusions that are made towards the end of the book – a sort of future history of Scottish football and a reimagined system and footballing landscape.

The story begins in the 19th century with the Scots who took the game around the world, who invented the passing game (known as combination play). I call this stage phase 1 in our footballing evolution. It's an important journey, at least for me it was, as it crystallised my thinking about the 'passing' game and how it came about and why others adopted it. Mainly it made me contemplate why we're not better at it today.

The story then moves on to look at 'phase 2' and the players who would go on to feature in the best club teams of the 20th century; and that's quite literally where the story ends! At least that's where the story of the great Scottish production line of footballing talent ends.

Where the story of our 'celebrated' history ends is, however, where a new one begins. The story of the 21st century begins with a discussion on the sea change that was sweeping through the game towards the end of the previous century. Around this time football was adjusting to the Bosman ruling; the effect of the ruling on youth football in Scotland was profound. Various initiatives and policies focused on youth development were brought in with little effect. Eventually Scotland would conduct its own review of Scottish football in 2010. Henry McLeish, the former First Minister of Scotland, would set out his blueprint for youth development in Scotland, most of which was implemented. Given that today's system is largely built in the image of McLeish's review, Chapters 4 and 5 are a kind of 'review of the review'. This provides an important discussion regarding some of the prevailing thinking and how these may be limiting factors that need to be addressed.

In Chapters 6 and 7, these discussions are developed in more detail in relation to how these and other policy decisions have affected player development and have contributed to the current state of youth football. The discussion and arguments are set against the scientific literature in relation to what's known about the process of player development, particularly when it comes to working with young people. It covers everything from our understanding of the concept of talent and talent identification, such as what's called the 'race to the bottom' (RTB) that characterises the process of identifying talented players at younger and younger ages.

It covers problems with selection, how and why selection errors are made. I chart the path we've taken to reach this point. A point that, as I go on to describe, is dependent on what I call a fatal error of a 'belief in *small numbers* and a dependency on a single pathway into the professional game'. The final section of the book is presented as a set of discussions, reflections, and questions. Organised in a such a way that key problems are summarised and potential solutions are proposed. Throughout the book I've tried to show as clearly as possible how I arrive at these lines of thought and the evidence I've used in support of them.

Final thought

Why did I write this book? Beyond the reasons already stated, I've been around Scottish football my whole life. I've discussed, debated, coached and been to hundreds of youth games. I've given lectures and presented at conferences on many of these topics. I have friends, colleagues and acquaintances who are involved in all aspects of youth sport; from those who coach kids at the weekend to professional coaches, from coach educators to Professors of Skill Acquisition. I have access to the scientific literature, much of which sits behind paywalls for those not involved in academia. For these reasons I have 'access to the story from an angle that not everyone has and therefore there is a sort of obligation to write it'. I stole that last line from Michael Lewis, who among other things wrote *Moneyball: The Art of Winning an Unfair Game*, and who has influenced some of the themes in this book. The truth is I heard him say something along those lines on a podcast while I was out cycling in 2019. He was speaking about his latest book, and it made me think about what story I have access to. Well, that story is this one and I hope you enjoy it!

Introduction – Defining
the landscape

WHEN WE talk about 'The System', we're essentially talking about the system for developing young players into future professional players. It is, however, more than this. Or at least within the context of this book it is. When people discuss the failings of our 'system', they're referring to the development of players who can elevate the game in Scotland. At least in the first place to the extent that would see us become regular qualifiers at major finals. In reality, as with most footballing nations, mere qualification isn't enough and nor should it be for Scotland.

Not just do we want to qualify for tournaments, we want to compete at them, and we want to do it with a brand of football that's admired and talked about. At least that's what I want and why this is the 'vision' that provides the backdrop for most of what will be discussed. To realise this vision, you need highly gifted and technical players; skilful, creative ones; flair players or even geniuses. Call it whatever you want. Many of these terms are used interchangeably to mean the same thing. The point is, it doesn't matter what you call it, you 'know it when you see it'!

Two problems jump out when this is your reference point for where we want to get to. First, we know we seldomly see this in our professional game; second, identifying what children from a population of tens of thousands have the potential to be these types of players is almost impossible – even if you think you 'know it when you see it', the evidence tells us that while this is true in youth football, it seldom progresses and persists into senior football.

The process of player development, as a field of interest in academic circles, falls under the umbrella term of what's known as Talent Identification and Development (TID). This field is that of studying the ways in which young people are identified and then developed, when the goal is to produce an elite-level performer. As such, the field looks at everything from problems with how children are selected for elite programmes, all the way through to how they're coached and beyond. In doing so it considers and investigates everything from the psychological aspects of development, social and financial factors, and the physical issues a person deals with as they travel through early adolescence and then on to adulthood. As we'll see, there's 'a lot is going on' in many different areas of a young person's life as they make these transitions.

Historically, TID is a process that was first formalised in training schools in Ancient Greece. The greatest success an athlete could achieve in the ancient world was to win an Olympic crown. Sport emerged out of the exercises used to prepare mind and body for war. Winners were special people, and to this extent the Athens school system was based on training young people to develop the physical, mental and moral attributes of its citizens.[1]

More recently, and from a scientific perspective, interest in TID has expanded considerably. More than 2,700 articles have been published on the subject between 1990 and 2019, 75 per cent of those in the last decade alone.[2] Scientific interest in the field of TID has arguably exploded due to the continued globalisation of sport and economic factors such as the potential return on investment if the outcome is successful. Not surprisingly, there are fears about the unrealistic expectations being placed on young people within some elite environments.

Whether preparing citizens for war in the ancient world or concerns regarding the pressure placed on young people for commercial gain, TID is a hot topic. At a governmental level it has been described as a 'global sporting arms race', where a disproportionate amount of money is apportioned to high-level sport. It has seen the creation of centres of excellence, performance schools and institutes of sport for the purposes of supporting the relatively few individuals who are selected for TID initiatives. More worryingly, it has in many instances led to the 'commercialisation' of what used to be young people's recreation time. The gradual tiptoe away from what used to be the game of the people, played on the street and accessible to all, has coincided with the demise of playing standards and changed the face of Scottish football.

The notion of 'The System', of course, is the central theme of this book. As we'll discuss shortly, the book identifies two systems of interest. When referring to the system it shouldn't be taken to mean the formal elite youth programmes run by professional clubs. That system is referred to throughout as System 1. The second, System 2, is the system for everyone else, those not in the elite system, essentially the system you need to get out of if you want to be a professional footballer.

In System 2 it's a race against time to be spotted before you run out of time and drop off the cliff of youth football. Every player knows that the time is coming, the time when you finally realise no professional club is coming to snap you up and propel you into a career as a professional. Perhaps it's not surprising that of the top ten most popular sports in Scotland, football has a higher rate of drop-out in 16–24-year-olds than any other.[3] A point in time before a footballer has even reached their peak.

As we'll come to see, time can be both your friend and enemy in youth football. From the time 'in the year' you were born to the time in your life you 'start' practising, to the amount of time you can practise and the timing of your maturity. Not to mention the minimum amount of time you get to be spotted, even though for most that time comes before they've even reached adulthood. It flies in the face of everything we know about the different rates of maturation and growth across a young person's lifespan. A lifespan that's characterised by unpredictable 'change' and transformations, when everything you thought you knew about a young person can turn out to be incorrect.

For a successful outcome to occur in System 1, two aspects of TID need to work to a high level if the system is to do what it sets out to do. That is, for System 1 to work we need to be good at the talent identification phase, and then good at the development phase. Get either part wrong and the system will malfunction. To get the initial part of the TID process right, the TI bit, we would need to somehow be operating in a world where the human eye is able to make predictions about the future that the most sophisticated computer and modelling systems couldn't achieve.

Today, despite faster and more powerful computers collecting data from remote satellites many times a day, the weather still can't be predicted accurately much beyond two weeks.[4] Yet when we select a ten-year-old for an academy programme we're trying to make a prediction about what they're going to be capable of ten years in the future. Not only that, but we've selected these players by excluding tens of thousands of other youngsters. Not surprisingly, TI on these terms is at best difficult, if not impossible. So difficult is it, that it has been shown that non-experts are as accurate as experts when it comes to spotting ability at a young age; even when experts look at the more mature form of the talent, they still aren't very good at predicting who will go on to excel at their sport in the future.[5]

We do tend to assume that we're good at the TI part, that from the tens of thousands of young people playing the game, we can spot the best ones. That's because we can. They're easy to spot. A kind of 'they've either got it, or they haven't' formula is good enough to spot the best ten-year-olds. By and large we believe that we've spotted all the talent, and few if any get missed. We do believe this, don't we? That if the talent is out there, we'll spot it! The cream always rises to the top, doesn't it? Well, if this is true, then we need to be honest with ourselves and admit that we're extremely poor at developing talent.

If not that then, there must be something inherently flawed in the talent development environment of Scottish football. As the book unfolds, both factors, the identification and development processes, are investigated further. Before we get too concerned about the development stage, we need to limit the number of errors and issues associated with the TI stage. We need to make sure that we aren't stacking the odds against ourselves before we even start the process of developing future players capable of enhancing our game. I'll present an argument in relation to how the current elite system is too narrow and limited in its reach. How it's affected by many factors such as issues around growth and maturity and social issues related to progressing in the game.

For the moment, though, on the notion of selection into elite programmes, Professor Joe Baker from York University in Canada – a world-leading researcher in the field of TID – asks: 'What would you do for talent selection if you assumed you were terrible at making these decisions instead of assuming you were good?' because you 'probably are wrong, because the evidence suggests you're terrible at making these decisions'.[6]

Assuming that we can address the errors and therefore issues with the TI phase, what then? Then we come to the development phase. Development never stops. Or at least it should never stop. Development is associated with improvement. For healthy development to take place there are a multitude of interconnected factors that will either facilitate or forestall it. These factors are both internal and external and need to be accounted for in our reimagining of player development in Scotland. Everything from fostering the intrinsic motivation needed to engage in activity for the many years to become good at it, to the environment and opportunities at the professional level of the game.

Everything from where we play to who we play against, to how we're coached, to factors that limit the rate of our development on our journey in the game.

So much talk about systems, yet so little understanding
Figures released in 2021 by the Scottish Youth Football Association (SYFA) showed that as many as 68,500 young people are registered players across more than 4,000 clubs.[7] All in all, when football at school is taken into account, that figure rises to around 200,000, of which around 2,500 are registered as youth players with professional clubs.[8] For the purposes of discussion, and as part of the organisational framework of the book, these numbers are then organised into the two systems previously mentioned – System 1 and System 2. This means that System 1 has around 2,500 participants, and System 2 somewhere in the region of 197,500 – assuming System 1 players are in this data.

A large part of System 1 is what's commonly known as the pro-youth set-up. Formally it's called Club Academy Scotland (CAS). The Scottish Football Association (SFA) partially funds and operates CAS for players from 11 years of age to U18. Clubs are audited based on factors such as domestic and international appearances for homegrown players, as well as factors such as the coaching qualifications and sport science provision at the clubs. The auditing process has led to the following categories that make up the CAS structure: an 'elite level' that consists of Aberdeen, Celtic, Dundee United, Hamilton Academical, Heart of Midlothian, Hibernian, Kilmarnock, Motherwell, Queen's Park, Rangers and St Mirren; followed by the 'performance (progressive) level' of Ayr United, Dundee, Dunfermline

Athletic, Greenock Morton, Inverness Caledonian Thistle, Partick Thistle, Ross County, St Johnstone; a 'performance level' of Livingston; and an 'advanced youth level' consisting of Airdrieonians, Alloa Athletic, Elgin City, Falkirk, Montrose, Queen of the South and Stirling Albion.[9]

That means the pro-youth structure in Scotland is made up of 27 clubs. Based on the available figures this would mean that, on average, professional clubs have over 90 players concurrently in their systems – probably around 15 per age group. The organisation of the different levels and age groups will differ across clubs, but they're all structured somewhat similarly. For example, at the time of writing, Celtic in the elite level have development centres for five years and above; a junior academy for U10s, U11s and U12s; an intermediate academy for U13s, U14s, U15s and U16s; and a professional academy for U18s.[10] Similarly, Stirling Albion in the bottom tier of CAS have age groups all the way from U8s to U17s.[11]

In addition to this, in 2012 the SFA launched its new Performance Schools programme on the back of former First Minister Henry McLeish's 'Review of Scottish Football'. The 'review' was to take a critical look at the way children were being identified, nurtured and developed. The performance schools were to link elite academies to education and signalled a new mindset in the pursuit of excellence. Essentially the schools were set up to give the most talented players more hours with a ball at their feet and what McLeish identified as the intensity of attention and provision needed if we're to produce players capable of elevating Scotland's fortunes on the pitch.[12] Today, each school has a full-time elite coach across their four years of schooling, and performance school attendees receive an extra 800 hours of coaching.[13] Many of the players in the CAS have an involvement with the SFA Performance School set-up. In Chapters 4 and 5, the discussion is set against McLeish's 'review' and the implications of its recommendation on player development today.

In System 1 there's an interconnection between pro clubs, performance schools and CAS. There's monitoring and assessment, all designed with the clear goal of producing 'the talent'. System 1 is what's typically known as a linear system, in which there are predefined stages and phases that children pass through. A sequential progression from one stage to another via a series of recognised steps. This means that the earlier a player is identified as having potential (or perhaps as being talented) the earlier they enter System 1 and the less likely they are to be left behind or missed out.

Entering System 1 comes with all the benefits associated with being in an elite programme and, as such, it's highly coveted. The clamour to be in System 1 has led to some concerns about the way the child is parented and the pressure and expectation placed on them at a young age. It can influence attitudes towards which boys' club a child plays for, perceptions of coaching standards, positions players play in (to showcase their talent), playing time afforded to a child, who the child's team-mates are and, crucially, how young a child begins their engagement with football.

It privileges the early developer (the good young player) and therefore places an emphasis on getting an 'early start'. In many respects this is driven by professional clubs who are engaging in the RTB when it comes to TI. That's to say, the age at which academies identify and select players is becoming younger and younger. In theory, if one team in an area, region or country starts to select at eight years old, then others need to follow suit; if another goes to seven, then they all need to move to seven. How low can you go, you might ask. This RTB of selecting children earlier and earlier in the professional system has happened in football clubs all around the world as they look to snap up the best 'talent' before anyone else.

This puts an emphasis on the effectiveness of your scouting system. In the Netherlands, Ajax are top of the tree when it comes to scouting. They're also revered for their ability to produce generational talent in a systematic fashion. According to Dutch journalist Michiel de Hoog, it's not that Ajax have one of the best academies in the world, what they have is one of the best talent identification scouting machines.[14] They're often able to get to the 'talent' before anyone else.

Therefore, to get in the slipstream of System 1 you need to start early. Consider this: if you're going to be good enough to get into a performance school at the age of 11 or 12, you'll probably have to have been good enough to be with a professional club since the age of nine or ten; to be good enough to be with a professional club since the age of nine or ten, you'll have to have been good enough to play for one of the better local teams in your area from the age of seven or eight; to be good enough to be in one of the better teams at seven or eight, you'll probably have to have been playing football for at least a couple of years before this.

For every child that starts early and shows the early promise to be selected into System 1 there are hundreds of late starters and late developers that can get locked out of the system at a very young age. A ten-year-old taking up the game today, could already be five years behind their early-starting counterpart, a developmental disadvantage that they're unlikely to claw back for several reasons that will be discussed in Chapter 5.

Nevertheless, the process for entry into System 1, in some form or another, begins with being 'scouted' from a young age. At the point of selection and progression into an elite academy programme a point of separation begins; your footballing landscape looks very different to that of those not selected. Being selected at the younger age brings all the advantages discussed and they quickly begin to multiply. System 1 players are 'hot-housed' into an elite environment, play best vs best fixtures and receive more intensive training and coaching than their System 2 counterparts. Soon, the accumulation of these factors means that it's not that difficult to stay ahead of their non-academy peers.

What then of System 2? For the purposes of this book, it's simply a term used to make a distinction between those in the pro-club system (System 1) and everyone else. If a formal system, such as System 1 is a coordinated and planned programme of development, where different support systems interact and connect to form a clear pathway, then System 2 is the opposite, essentially a non-system of largely unconnected parts. It includes the grassroots participation system run by the SYFA, and everything else that's available to a young person or otherwise.

A lot of good work goes on in different elements of System 2. Grassroots and participation football is well organised across the various regions. At a grassroots level football is largely run by volunteers, from coaches to club secretaries, from treasurers to first-aid officers, and everything in between. Very often parents will fill the various roles needed to make sure the clubs continue to function. There are extensive age-group leagues and cup competitions. It's where football takes place on a mass-participation level; however, when it comes to being young, with aspirations of being a professional footballer, it's something of a no-man's land. To be clear, a massive amount of organisation and interest is involved in System 2. The reason for making the distinction is for the best part that there's a single pathway into elite football, and it's via System 1.

In System 2 then, it's less formal. Players can get out of and back into the system whenever they like. As players get older and their interests change, or they just get fed up, they'll often take a break from playing. It's not unusual to see them reappear playing for the same or another team when it suits them. Players can move more freely from one team to another. Often players will move team to play alongside friends or they simply want a change or to play for a better team. There are multiple entry and exit points. The door is never locked behind you in System 2 – there's a revolving door.

This level of flexibility and autonomy has the hallmarks of what's called a non-linear system. When it comes to the science, a mass-participation non-linear system has all the potential to produce the quality and quantity of players needed to elevate the game. As will be argued later,

System 1 has much to learn from System 2 – not the other way round.

Commercialisation of kids' fitba

The next part of The System that we will talk about seems to have emerged out of the demise of what many consider to be one of the main factors that produced so many great Scottish football players. With the demise of the street as a place of play and with concerns over how children spend their free time, there has been a rise in the commodification of kids' sport by adults. This seems to have coincided with increased parental awareness of how entry to System 1 works.

The number of players at a grassroots level in Scotland has attracted entrepreneurial thinking, and children's involvement in football is now an industry. This now means that, if you can afford it, your child can access extra and more specialised coaching. Not only that but many of these companies offer pathways that share similarities with the elite-level structure. For example, Coerver Coaching is a global coaching company created in 1984, which has an active franchise in Scotland. Coerver advertises itself as having 'the UK's Premier Grassroots Player Development programme for Boys & Girls'. According to its website it has a performance academy at 'development', 'advanced' and 'elite' levels'.

To determine the level you enter the academy, a 'trial' is required to test an individual's ability in relation to skill, speed, sense, strength and spirit.[15] They also, at cost, have an elite development squad programme in partnership with Benfica FC.[16] In some respects, the commercial sector has mimicked elements of the pro-youth System 1 and to an extent appeals to those kids who are looking to supplement their current training programmes to heighten their chances of entering System 1.

However, all this comes at a cost, and in some ways has begun to drive the game away from its working-class roots. For example, there are fears that football is fast becoming something for those who can afford it. Andy McLaren, the former Dundee United player, runs sessions for kids from the most deprived areas of Glasgow who can't afford to pay for football. According to McLaren, 'These are areas guys like Kenny Dalglish, Frank McAvennie, Bertie Auld [came from]; really, we could be missing out on the next Kenny Dalglish because he's not got a fiver a week.'[17]

What's for sure is that, increasingly, and more than any generation before them, children's ongoing participation in sport (football or otherwise) is likely to be facilitated by some form of coaching. This early adult involvement in young person development may greatly impact on the player the child becomes. For good or bad, this issue needs to be part of the wider conversation. The goal of this chapter isn't to look at the various elements of System 1 or 2 in any more detail than already expressed. This will be looked at later in the book. However, the argument stated here and that will be developed further as the book progresses is this: if the fortunes of Scottish clubs and our national team are to improve, both System 1 and 2 need to be considered as viable talent pools.

Currently they're not. Instead, we have largely a one-system (System 1) pathway, and we've designed it that way. Perhaps based on some reasonably plausible logic. It's plausible, yet not backed up by evidence, to assume that if you sweep up the most talented players at as early an age as possible, expose them to the best facilities and coaches, reduce the numbers so the fewer (but most talented players) get more resources spent on them, that the outcome will be better players at a point sometime in the future, and yet this simply isn't working.

The Scottish Football League system

The last piece of the footballing landscape that needs to be discussed is the progression out of the age-group systems and into adult football. Until 2013 it was impossible for clubs in regional leagues to progress into the national leagues, as Scotland had no pyramid system to create such a pathway. The current pyramid system is comprised of tier 1, the Scottish Premier League (SPL), while tiers 2–4 are the Scottish Football League (SFL). Below this sit the non-league and regional leagues that make up tiers 5–10. The relevance of this to a discussion about The System is that this is the pathway, alongside U20 amateur football, from age-group boys' football into adult football. Many boys' clubs in System 2 will have adult teams in tiers 5–10, especially if the club is working its way through the SFA's club accreditation scheme. In this respect several now promote a pathway from age-group football into their first teams.

For those at professional clubs, the 2022/23 season saw the return of the SPFL Reserve League, which is largely the next step for those in the elite system progressing out of age-group competition. Alongside this there's a proposal to introduce a new Conference League into the pyramid system. This will potentially become a tier 5 league and is proposed to be made up of a combination of professional clubs and current tier 5 teams. This is the evolution of the move that saw the B teams of Celtic, Rangers and Hearts compete in the Lowland League. The move is to continue to explore how the so-called development gap is bridged between the ages of 17 and 21, essentially the gap between youth- and first-team football for those with professional clubs.

Whatever structure is settled on, once again the focus and attention continue to be disproportionately focused on the System 1 'talent', a strategy that I'll argue is flawed on many levels. As the journalist and broadcaster Stuart Cosgrove points out:

> One of the primary arguments in support of B teams being in the league is the holy grail of youth development – that Scotland's best youngsters will push forward in a notoriously difficult career path. It is a noble ambition pitted with contradiction – what about talent not part of the gilded four? Why, if developing Scottish talent is the objective, do the clubs that have been privileged sign so many players from elsewhere?[18]

Everything up to this point in the life of a System 1 player is set up to allow their talent to flourish. There's opportunity everywhere if you've come through System 1, that's until you attempt to make the progression to senior first-team football. Now the landscape has started to shift. The top clubs are at a loss with what to do next. In many respects the notion of a first-team pathway is nothing more than an idealistic slogan that reflects what should happen if the system was functioning correctly. This situation is addressed more fully in Chapter 8.

Section 1 – Past

Chapter 1

The modern history of Scottish football – phase 1

THE INTRODUCTION set out the landscape of youth football in modern Scotland. It was in no way an exhaustive characterisation. Nor was it meant to be. More a rough sketch, an outline and a point of reference for much of the discussion in the later parts of the book. The task in hand now is to connect the conversation across the 'systems' of the past, present and hopefully the future to help inform us how we might start to think of a new future for youth football in Scotland. As such, this section of the book looks at Scottish football from a historical perspective to understand its earliest phases and subsequent evolution. When this stage is overlooked, misleading conclusions are often drawn. The goal of this section isn't to give a history lesson on what once was, rather it's to use the historical perspective to sharpen our vision of the present.[1]

The Scottish game has arrived at where it is today as a process of more than 150 years of adaptation and change. Not only has the world of football changed, but the world around us and our role in it has also changed. Scotland, despite being Europe's poorest independent country in 1700, would go on to create the ideals of modern life and take these ideals around the world; by the beginning of the 18th century Scotland had become Europe's first literate society with a cultural bias towards reading, learning and education, and in the process would become a global powerhouse in industries such as shipping and the tobacco trade.[2]

Scotland is illustrious in its endeavours of an intellectual nature, responsible for inventions such as the telephone, television, radar, the steam engine – a Scot even invented the Bank of England and the dugout. More significantly, on the pitch itself, and as we'll go on to discuss, Scots pioneered dribbling the ball and passing it, which created a more expansive style of football that would be labelled as 'combination play'. This style of play pioneered by the Scots is one that's widely adopted today.

The Scottish fast-paced passing play also employed for the first time position-specific players, changing the formation of the game in England. Clubs would recruit Scots and organised matches against Scottish teams in a conscious attempt to emulate and learn from them. This deliberate move to adopt the Scottish model changed the game south of the border to such an extent that by the late 1880s the majority of clubs in England were working class, like those in Scotland.

We have a propensity for driving change and for progress. Globally, Scots have punched above their weight, especially when you consider there's only around five and a half million of us. We've adapted and refused to accept our circumstances. According to the sports journalist Hugh McIlvanney, Scots have a collective self-assurance about them, they refuse to be belittled or taken for granted.[3] Not surprisingly then, this current and ongoing decline in our ability to excel at our national game hurts. We might not readily admit it, but it's a source of shame to us – it's a national embarrassment! We've arrived here as part of a slow process that crept up on us when we weren't looking and seemingly took root before we could do anything about it.

From a historical perspective, the World Cup finals in 1998 are an important landmark. The roots of our decline had already started to bed in, we just didn't know it yet. When Craig Brown and his Scotland team exited the Stade Geoffroy-Guichard on 23 June 1998 they brought the curtain down on what I'll go on to discuss as 'phase 2' in our footballing evolution. After an opening defeat to Brazil and a 1-1 draw with Norway, a 3-0 defeat to Morocco knocked Scotland out of the tournament. The century had ended, once again, with Scotland failing to qualify out of the group stages of a major tournament. It was little consolation at the time that this was our sixth appearance out of the previous seven tournaments. We know only too well that six more World Cup finals have come and gone since, and Scotland have failed to qualify for all of them. Scotland hold the dubious distinction, alongside Hungary, of being the only current international team to have played in eight World Cup finals but none in the 21st century.[4]

There's a sense of now or never when it comes to Scottish football. When it comes to the powerhouse footballing leagues, we know we're cut adrift as a matter of our geography and appeal. We can do little about that (although Celtic and Rangers have talked about jumping the geographical ship over the years). We don't, however, need to be cut off when it comes to producing world-class players and teams. Scotland did it before, and as we'll come to see they did it at scale; during one semi-final stage of the European Cup in the 80s, across the four teams participating, 30 per cent of the players were Scottish. For now, I'll leave you guessing on that one, but the point is we did it before and we can do it again. Before we get back to how, let's look at the 19th century to discuss some important factors in phase 1 of our evolutionary history.

The modern history of Scottish football – phase 1

To look at something from a historical perspective you need to establish an entry point. The first documentation of football in Scotland goes back to 1424, to an act of parliament of James I forbidding the playing of the game.[5] To what extent this deterred Scots from playing the game isn't clear. Records from the time are brief and lack specifics. However, by the early 1700s the 'common people of Scotland' were described as addicted to the game of football.[6] What's clear is that between James I's reign and early Victorian times some form of football was being played in Scotland.[7] While it's unclear what form(s) of the game that was, there are no records to suggest that the modern form of the game, known as the rugby football game, was played until after 1850.[8] For the purposes of this book, and by way of an entry point, this is where the story of the modern history of Scottish football begins.

Perhaps unsurprisingly, nowhere could modern football be seen more clearly than in Glasgow. The arrival of the modern game in Scotland, via the private schooling system, coincided with the population of Glasgow doubling between

1851 and the early 1900s.[9] When Hampden Park opened in 1903, and alongside Celtic Park and Ibrox, the city had the three biggest stadiums in the world, capable of housing almost half of the city's population.[10] The commentator R.M. Connell, writing in 1906, argued that 'the enthusiasm of the Scot for the Association game is without parallel in any race for any particular sport or pastime'.[11]

Post 1850, this enthusiasm is notable for two key factors, and it's through these factors that I'll discuss this part of our history. First, the story of the enthusiasm for the game in Scotland is inseparable from the story of the development of the game around the world; and second, is the style of football pioneered and exported by the Scots. It's a style that, today, is associated with what we consider the beautiful game. There's simply no doubt that Scottish players and coaches have played a major role in, and influenced, the development of the game worldwide. According to Michael Grant and Rob Robertson, authors of *The Management: Scotland's Great Football Bosses*, Scots working abroad introduced the passing game in countries such as Germany, France, Italy, Argentina, Uruguay, Brazil and Mexico.

The son of a Scotsman is said to have been present at the birth of football in Brazil. When Charles Miller travelled to join his father in Brazil, legend has it that among his luggage was a football and a copy of the Hampshire FA rules of the game. Miller was born in Brazil to a Scottish father and Brazilian mother of British descent.[12] At the age of nine he was sent to England to continue his schooling at the Bannister Court School in Southampton.[13] On his return in 1894, Miller picked two teams of men from the local gas company, the London and Brazilian Bank and Sao Paulo Rail Company. The men contested what's widely regarded as the first game of football of the modern era in Brazil. Miller would be influential in setting up the Liga Paulista 1901 that gave birth to association football in the country. Six years later Scotland's influence in the country was further enhanced when the former Ayr United defender Jock Hamilton took over at Club Athletico Paulistano and became Brazil's first professional coach.[14] Not only this, but he reputedly would also lay the foundations for future success by putting in place a coaching structure that was used throughout Brazilian football from youth level upwards.[15]

Elsewhere in South America, Alexander Hutton, a former teacher from Glasgow, moved to Argentina to work at the St Andrews Scottish school in Buenos Aires and is said to have set up the inaugural Argentinian league in 1893.[16] Before then, Hutton had set up his own English School in Buenos Aires where he quickly installed a football pitch. He brought the first leather footballs to Argentina; the odd-looking deflated pieces of stitched leather had bemused customs officials and his staff at the school, who struggled to see what use they were to be put to. Hutton would go on to form a team, Alumni Athletic Club, that would win ten league titles and become Argentina's first great club; this feat has only been surpassed by the *cinco grandes* ('big five'): Racing Club de Avellaneda, River Plate, Independiente, Boca Juniors, and San Lorenzo de Almagro.[17] Such was his influence that Argentine sportswriter Félix Frascara described Hutton as the 'Father of Argentine Football'.[18]

These aren't isolated examples of the Scottish influence on the game worldwide. John Harley, an engineer from Springburn in Glasgow, played for and then managed Peñarol in Uruguay. Harley and José Piendibene were the two exceptional players in the great pre-war Peñarol team. Notably, Harley, who captained the team for eight years, taught those around him the passing game.[19] In recognition of its Scottish roots, the short methodical passing game came to be known as 'a la escosesa', and this contrasted with the other style of play that was tutored in the country at the time – the 'kick and rush' game of England.[20] According to Uruguayan academic Rafael Bayce, this influence was paid back in cruel style when Uruguay crushed Scotland 7-0 at the 1954 World Cup finals in Switzerland.[21]

Even before football had taken root in Latin America and Continental Europe, it was being played in Asia. Football arrived in British Burma in 1879 when James George Scott from Dairsie in Fife introduced football to the country during his 25 years as a colonial official there.[22] Earlier than this, around 1870, John Prentice, a Beattock-born, Greenock-educated engineer, introduced a modernised form of the game in China.[23] In North America, David Forsyth from Perthshire introduced football in Canada at Berlin High School in 1870. He helped set up the first leagues that would spread locally before he played an instrumental role in the formation and administration of the Western Football Association.[23]

The story of the introduction of football into any nation is, of course, open to interpretation and depends on who is telling the story. The truth is always more complex than the simplistic creation of legendary figures and stories of the founding fathers. It's more realistic to suggest that no nation can claim to have invented football, that the pioneers of football in South America were likely South Americans with German, Italian and Swiss as well as British influence, and that this was connected to intercultural empire and nation-building, to industrialisation, trade and shipping, and travel, and the educational reform associated with this.[24,25] What's clearer is that the Scots had a profound influence on the way the game would go on to be played. Some of the historical figures mentioned, alongside many more influential Scots, became known collectively as 'the Scotch Professors'.

As well as the pioneers of passing the ball and of 'combination' play, the Scots were also the originators of dribbling the ball and were among the first professionally paid players. High-profile Scottish professional players such as James Love and Fergus Suter from Glasgow were paid to play for the Lancashire club, Darwen, against Old Etonians in the 1879 FA Cup Final; and Peter Andrews and James Laing were paid to play for the Heeley Club in Sheffield – men such as these are said to have been derogatorily labelled as the 'scotch professors' by the 'high priests' of amateurism.[26]

Eric Dunning, the former Emeritus Professor of Sociology at the University of Leicester, speculated that this label had been given to the Scots 'on account of what they had to teach the English about the game as it was constituted in those days, as well as the fact that they were illegitimately paid'.[26] According to Scottish football historian Ged O'Brien, this onset of professionalism weakened the game in Scotland as English scouts started to flood into the big towns and cities to entice players south to train players and clubs in this new style of football. The 'scotch professors' moved south and then eventually to the continent of Europe and beyond to teach the passing and running game to the world.[27]

Author and historian Ian Campbell Whittle hypothesises that the early history of Scottish football, and the Scottish style, can be traced to shinty-playing footballers of the 1870s, the devastating effect of the potato famine that hit Europe in the 1840s causing large numbers of people to move. While Ireland was worst hit, the Highlands of Scotland weren't far behind. People had to flee to survive. Areas such as Renfrewshire, Lanarkshire and Dunbartonshire were taking in as many people annually as Glasgow.[28]

These areas were experiencing a population explosion. The footballing hotbed of the Vale of Leven in Dunbartonshire was one such place. While the highlanders came to work in the local factories, they also brought with them the game of shinty. Soon shinty was being played in Alexandria, Renton and Dumbarton, and before long was reputed to have the largest following of all sports in the area. Significantly, the shinty players decided to give football a try but knew little of the rules or conventions of the game. While association football had only broken away from 'rugby football' in 1871, the year before the formation of the Vale of Leven Athletic and Football Club, it wouldn't have mattered much to the young highlanders, who knew little of either codes.[29]

This population explosion of people ambivalent to the conventions of the game may well have been the perfect storm for the emergence of the Scottish style of play. According to Campbell Whittle the source of this new philosophy was the Vale of Leven, and the catalyst was the sport of shinty, a game of not only lofted long passes but also a combination of short passes, trapped and passed along the ground, and of triangles.

The genesis of this new style aside, for the Scots the combination play would prove to be the perfect antidote when they came up against the greater physicality of their English counterparts. English football was more associated with a fast-paced kick-and-rush style – partly to do with the early rules of the game – something more akin to rugby than the soccer we know today. The English style of play of the day seems to have been shaped by their greater physicality and the rules of the game. As Jonathan Wilson writes in his book *Inverting the Pyramid*, rules varied from place to place and were loosely structured around the objective of getting a roughly spherical object to a target at opposing ends of a notional pitch.[30]

Up until 1863, carrying the ball with the hands was still practised, hacking was part of the game, such rule's meaning that football was typically a running and kicking game with some individual dribbling. English teams relied on individualism and physical strength, a key tactic being the practice of 'backing-up' that had flourished due to the absence of an offside rule.[31] This involved as many as eight forwards who would line up to forge an attack using raw brawn and dribbling skills. Breakdowns in play would be supported by a muscular rearguard who would look to quickly regain possession and launch a new attack. When done well, a large physical team was a daunting proposition to play against. All this conjures up images of the game we now more associate with rugby.

According to the sports historian Andy Mitchell, the marked physical discrepancies between English and Scottish players was evident in the first international between the two teams in 1872, played at the West of Scotland cricket ground in Partick. The visitors lined up in something resembling a 1-2-7 formation; Mitchell surmises that the Scottish style of dribbling and passing the ball to create a more expansive style of football was clearly alien to the English, who had been brought up playing as individuals who relied on a strong physical presence – in contrast to the combination play of the Scots. The *Glasgow Herald* report from the game noted: 'The Englishmen had all the advantage of weight, their average being about two stones heavier than the Scotchmen and they had also the advantage in pace. The strong point of the home club [*sic*] was that they played excellently well together.'[32]

In the match, Scotland were represented by Queen's Park, and given the weight advantage, most commentators expected an England victory, but it finished goalless, a scoreline that wouldn't be repeated for over a century. The theory behind this 'scientific approach' was that the best way to combat physicality was to tire the opposition out to neutralise their physical advantage. At some point in the match opposition players would become fatigued (perhaps physically and mentally), make a mistake, or could be picked off and exploited accordingly.

As with many great inventions and endeavours the genesis for creativity is the need to solve a problem. Combination play, if patiently adhered to, would eventually pay dividends but only if the application of the approach was adopted by all. To complement this style of play, the Scots, as well as pioneering systematic passing, were the first to give each player an allocated position; so effective was this approach that it would change the way opposition teams lined up against Scottish teams – forward players were reduced from seven to five and the number of defenders increased to five or six.[33]

The Scots had a distinct advantage when it came to gaining a head start in relation to this new, preferred and revered style of football. The rules of the game were so disparate from region to region that it promoted a particular style of play in one place, and something different elsewhere. Queen's Park, as the arbitrators of the rules at the time in Scotland, would play many of their early fixtures in matches among themselves. Up until 1873 and the formation of the SFA, Queen's Park were the game's governing body. Unlike the English, according to Wilson, on Queens Park's establishment in 1867 they adopted a version of the offside law that was more conducive to passing than either the FA's first offside law or its revision in 1866. Queen's Park would eventually accept the FA's version around 1870, but by this time their passing style was very much embedded in their playing. This advantage had been embedded due to a lack of matches in Scotland around the time, so Queen's Park essentially 'hot-housed' their talent and played many matches against themselves.

Whatever its origins, the combination style of play would supersede the kick-and-rush style and, as can be seen with Harley's 'a la escosesa', it would be exported around the world by the Scotch Professors. These early styles of play are associated with the inequalities of the 18th and 19th centuries, where social class accounted for a 2cm difference in height, serving as an indication of the health status between the well-off and less well-off.[34] From the 1870s in the west of Scotland, the epicentre of the game, working-class football clubs had sprung into life, while in England all the leading clubs, and a such the national team, were made up entirely of men from middle-class and upper-middle-class backgrounds.[35]

Reflections – the lost art of passing

The objective of this chapter wasn't to reminisce about the past, it was to sharpen our vision of the present. First, the matter of physicality. Today, in the 21st century, Scottish men are the smallest in the United Kingdom, averaging 5ft 8in, while across the world the Dutch are the tallest at 6ft.[36, 37] Gordon Strachan once cited 'genetics' as a factor in Scotland's failure to qualify for the 2018 World Cup finals. According to Strachan, the issue of height was a recurring factor, leading to the off-the-cuff remark that 'genetically we have to work at things, maybe we get big women and men together and see what we can do'.[38]

To date the scientific literature hasn't found a link between the recruitment of taller players and greater success on the football pitch. The average height of the Scotland team for the final qualifying match for the 2018 World Cup finals was 181cm, very similar to the average height of 181.7cm of players who would go on to contest the 2018 World Cup finals; notably, the average height of players from France was 180.5cm, Brazil 180.4cm, Spain 179.5cm and Argentina 179.4 cm. The Netherlands, who also failed to qualify for the 2018 finals, were the tallest team in the world around this time with an average height of 183cm.[39]

However, unlike Strachan's team, the Scottish players of the 19th century (and the 20th) used these inequalities to their advantage – as did Strachan himself as a player. The expansive combination play of the Scotch Professors was designed to destabilise more physical opponents, which has parallels with the modern idea of 'positional play'. According to Pep Guardiola, perhaps its most successful exponent, the aim is to 'move the opponent, not the ball', emphasising the importance of interconnectedness and teamwork, and the philosophy is executed via the creation of triangles, diamonds and short passes, such as is associated with the combination play of the Scotch Professors.[40]

When we consider the so-called physical inequalities of the early Scots, it may come as no surprise that when Guardiola's Barcelona dominated football in 2008/9, he did so with a group of players who were physically diminutive. That year Barcelona won the Champions League, La Liga and the Copa del Rey, scoring 194 goals in 73 matches. Of his regular attacking players that year, only Thierry Henry was over 1.8 metres tall, wile Pedro, Xavi, Andres Iniesta, Lionel Messi, and Samuel Eto'o were all smaller, averaging 1.75 metres.[41] Currently the average height of an English premiership player is over 1.82 metres.[42]

Much like Guardiola's Barcelona team, what the Scotch Professors lacked in weight and height they made up for in speed of play and technique. In introducing the 'pass' and combination play the Scots had transformed the game into an art form. The players who were the best exponents were those who could not only dribble the ball but could also 'give and take' a pass.[43] More than anything, today we seem to have lost the *art of passing* and all that's involved in that. This might come as a surprise; you would only need to observe an elite youth session to see that it's not something that's neglected on the training pitch, and yet we've become such ineffective exponents of it.

While Strachan's 'genetics' comments were tongue in cheek, there's a more developed line of thought behind them. According to Strachan, to play passing football, players not only need to be comfortable on the ball and be able to pass it, but they also need to be willing and able to take the ball in any situation, to be able to shield the ball and, if need be, beat a player, and for that you need core strength. According to Strachan:

> Barcelona and Man City, all the top teams ... they call them passing teams ... but when you watch them ... everyone in Barcelona and everyone in Man City can beat you: that doesn't happen in Scottish football, if it gets to a position where someone is coming to close you down, you play it long, or you play it first time and hope it gets there, the top players [rather than gamble with it] can shield it or they can beat you.[44]

Strachan highlights that this needs a change in mentality in relation to coaching and messaging to players. Players need to be encouraged to be responsible for the ball, encouraged to beat a player rather than get rid of it. This requires a de-emphasis on the notion that you must not get 'caught on the ball' – all these attributes are commonly found in the great passing teams. However, while I agree that we need to develop the attributes and mentality to play this way, I feel we're missing an ingredient, and that's what the historical perspective enlightens us about.

The Scotch Professors, and those who came after, developed the passing game as a 'solution to a problem', not because it looked pretty. What became the 'beautiful game' was born out of necessity – the classic 'problem' first, 'solution' second conditions that can be found at the birth of any great innovation. For the Scots it was to combat a more physical opponent and to play to their own strengths; for Guardiola the problem was to move the opponent, to create an overload and then to exploit the space this created. The solution would come to be known as the 'tiki-taka' style and, much like 'combination play', these were labels given to describe what others were observing.

For now, the historical perspective leaves us with food for thought for the future, particularly how we go about introducing this competency back into our talent system. One thing for sure is that you need to know 'why' you're passing the ball, and not just be drilled to do so!

Numbers game – a shrinking talent population

The second factor that should sharpen our vision of the present, and a factor that I'll return to later in the book, is the issue of numbers. The size of your talent pool matters. It really matters! In 1851, the population of Scotland was 18 per cent that of England and Wales.[45] Today it has fallen to around half of that, but not only that – by comparison to England we have an older population.[46] More revealing is the sharp decline in the birth of males per year over the last 170 years.

The players who contested the first Scotland versus England game in 1872 were born between 1844 and 1852.[47] On average across those nine years there were just under 50,000 male births in Scotland per year (the peak year being in 1847 with 58,000); by way of comparison, from 2000 to 2021 the average males born per year was just under 28,000 (the highest being 30,570 in 2008).[48] Scotland's decline on the football pitch correlates with the declining number of males born per year. The Lisbon Lions were born between 1930 and 1944, when on average there were over 46,000 males born per year; the decorated players of the 1982 World Cup finals, who we'll discuss in the next chapter, were born across an era of an average of more than 48,000 males born per year.

In addition to this is another factor that wasn't an issue in the 19th century, or the best part of the 20th century – in today's society, more than 16 per cent of 2–15-year-olds are obese.[49] This is a barrier to participation that shrinks the talent pool even further. This issue needs to be taken seriously when it comes to thinking about the structure and make-up of Systems 1 and 2. A smaller talent pool has implications on many levels. Fewer people playing, less competition for places, a smaller margin for error when selecting. The issue of small numbers is a key issue, and as we'll come to see, it's a recurring theme, one that's hurting us, but in some ways it's self-inflicted. We need to design a 'system' that minimises this issue but instead we have a system that exacerbates it – more than anything it's the pool that's too small, not the players!

What's clear and what does matter is that style of play emerged out of the 'mix' of cultural constraints of the time. The question of most relevance then becomes: when, how and where did we lose this philosophy? If Scotland exported the passing game to the world then why did so many nations retain this style? The passing game continues to be synonymous with the beautiful game. Its best exponents are the best players in the world, and they tend to play for the best teams. These questions need to be addressed. Before we get to that, though, we draw the curtain on phase 1 of our modern footballing history and head to the 20th century, a century that for the best part would see the Scottish player and manager flourish at the highest levels of European football ... and a Scotland team capable of winning the World Cup!

Chapter 2

The modern history of Scottish football – phase 2

PICKING UP where we left off then, 'combination' play was brought on by the inequalities of being born and raised in the north versus the more affluent south, a style of play that was an adaptation to combat the physical nature of our more brutish neighbours and the rules of the game at the time. The environment of your developmental upbringing and the adaptation to these conditions are fundamental to who we are and what we've become. Nowhere can the environmental influences shaping our development be seen more clearly than in the Scotland of the early 20th century and the social conditions that prevailed at the time. If matters on the pitch and the rules had 'most' shaped what we talk about from the 19th century, it was matters off the pitch that would have the biggest influence on our story of football in the 20th century – a period where being Scottish and good at football went hand in hand.

A sense of social injustice would seem to be the driving force in the lives of the 'ordinary people' of Scotland in the first half of the century. For example, despite there being two million people unemployed at the beginning of the 1930s, two thousand people attended the wedding of Lady Margaret and Mr James Drummond Hay in Perth.[1] Much of the unemployment was centred around our biggest population centres. According to Adam Powley, collective survival was stitched into the fabric of life, and, at the time, football was seen as a way out of the drudgery and physical hardship of tough manual work; the ticket out of this life towards better prospects appeared to drive a desire to hone skills and to learn the game.[2]

Given such cultural hardship, a strange anomaly exists to this day. When Scotland play football people make their way to Hampden from all over Scotland to sing songs about kings, warriors and battles – a time when Scotland was controlled by the decisions of elites and a tiny group of powerful people. There seems to be no place for the story of the ordinary lives, of the agricultural labourers whose back-breaking work formed the landscapes, or indeed the work of those who built Scotland and the great churches, castles and grand houses.[3] It was the working man and the cultural condition of their upbringing that built not only a footballing nation but many world-leading industries.

The only obvious connection is that Scottish football and Scottish history are somewhat intertwined in terms of raised expectations and glorious failure. In 1314 a Scottish army led by Robert the Bruce defeated an English army of almost twice its size at Bannockburn, but such victories were followed by devastating defeats at Flodden in 1513 and Culloden in 1746.[4] Much of Scotland's history, according to Gordon A. Craig, the Scottish-American historian, can be characterised as a tale of turbulence and violence and of feckless gallantry and lost causes.[5] Today, I'm sure we would agree this is an acceptable characterisation of the highs and lows of Scottish football during the century.

It's undeniable, though, that it was hardship that would shape many of our all-time-great footballing figures. Bill Shankly worked down the pits before earning a full-time professional contract, so too did Sir Matt Busby and Jock Stein. Sir Alex Ferguson was a Clydeside tool maker and a trade unionist. What appears to have united them was a determination that they were never going back. There's a general acceptance that their early experiences shaped the great managers they would go on to become. In Scottish society, nowhere can the driving force of cultural hardship be seen more clearly than on the football pitch. However, as we'll go on to talk about, by the end of the century the lights would go out on this great period and to date they haven't been turned back on.

Leading up to the turn of the century, the gradual decline of Queen's Park had started with the rise and rise of what would become our footballing powerhouses of Rangers and Celtic. This coincided with English players growing ever more resentful of the growing number of Scots playing in England. The Scotch Professors were branded by some as traitors and base mercenaries.[6] It was becoming clear that a Scottish league with more fixtures was going to be needed.

In March 1890, at the request of Renton chairman Peter Fairly, a meeting was held in Holton's Commercial Hotel in Glasgow.[7] At the time, Renton were one of Scotland's biggest teams. They had won the Football World Championships in 1888 by beating FA Cup holders West Bromwich Albion. Renton's most notable player was their captain James Kelly, who, according to John Cairney, was the first 'total footballer' of the modern era – a 'pivot who linked defence to attack'. A player 'so good' that the capture of Kelly by Celtic a year later was so significant that many believe he was fundamental in attracting supporters away from Hibernian and towards the newly formed Glasgow club.[8] In August of 1890 the first Scottish League fixtures took in a league contested by 11 clubs. Ironically, Renton were expelled from the league, accused of professionalism. While they returned to the league in 1891, they struggled financially and eventually resigned in 1897.

Returning then to matters of the 20th century. For the best part it would be a century known for producing some of the greatest football managers of all time, as well as teams that would flourish wherever they played, and as a time when the services of Scottish players were in high demand. This was the century in which the game had 'formally' become professional. As the century progressed, football players would become the heroes of the working class, someone who would give fans a heightened sense of themselves in a language they understood.[9] The game was an opportunity to break free from the working-class straitjacket, it offered the prospect of a better life. According to Tom Fagan, who manged Albion Rovers in the 1980s: 'The miners were hungry, hungry boys and the only way they could get away from where they were, to get out of the pits, was through football, and they could get on to playing for ten pounds a week which was a fortune then. Full time ... my God!'[10]

In England alone, between 1946 and 1981, 1,653 Scots played in the English league, while simultaneously making up the majority of players playing in the Scottish League.[11]

This was a boom time for Scottish players, and young men could see role models everywhere they looked in their communities. So prolific was it for producing footballers, that the area in and around Bellshill was referred to as the 'unofficial' capital of Scottish football. There was an attitude of 'if you can, then I can'. The social and cultural conditions of Scotland were a potent mix, and it created a system that looked like it would keep producing a never-ending flow of top-class footballers.

Phase 2 – the 20th century on the pitch

It's unknown at what exact point in Scotland's footballing past that 'the system' for producing top-class football players became broken. But there can be little doubt that the pipeline is broken. No further reminder is needed that Scotland last qualified for a World Cup finals in 1998, but when did the decline really begin and what caused it? You, perhaps like me, were brought up on tales of the great Scottish players who graced the game. Particularly the many great players who plied their trade in England. Far from being in decline, there was an extended period when Scottish players were on the up and in high demand. From the dominant Arsenal team of the 1930s, starring the 'wee wizard' Alex James, to the Billy Bremner-powered Leeds United team of the 1960s. While at Manchester United, Denis Law is the only man to have two statues dedicated to him, one at the Stretford End concourse, the other overlooking the stadium's forecourt, where he's immortalised as part of the 'United Trinity' alongside George Best and Sir Bobby Charlton.[12] Dave Mackay, John White and Bill Brown all featured prominently in the Tottenham Hotspur team that won the first league and cup double of the modern era in 1960/61.[13]

On the home front, Scottish teams were a force to be reckoned with in Europe. It's well documented that Celtic won the European Cup in 1967, becoming the first British team to do so. Before this, Hibernian were the first British team to play in Europe's premier club competition, reaching the semi-finals in 1955. Five years later Rangers lost in the semi-finals of the European Cup to Eintracht Frankfurt, who would go on to contest perhaps the most famous final of them all against Real Madrid at Hampden Park. A year later Rangers reached their first European final, losing to Fiorentina over two legs in the Cup Winners' Cup.

Celtic reached the semi-finals of the same tournament in 1964 and 1966 before their immortalised triumph in the Estádio Nacional in Lisbon on 25 May 1967. The Lisbon Lions are celebrated for many reasons, not least because of the geographical proximity to Glasgow from which the players came. Jock Stein, as Scottish sport writer Hugh McIlvanney put it, won the 'European Cup with a Glasgow District XI'.[14] Not only was every player born within a 30-mile proximity of Celtic Park, but all but one grew up within ten miles of the stadium.[15]

Less than a week after Celtic's triumph, in the Städtisches Stadion in Nuremberg, Rangers were narrowly beaten by Bayern Munich in the final of the Cup Winners' Cup. A disallowed goal for Rangers in regulation time sent the match into extra time. Franz Roth's winner was enough to secure the German team's first European trophy.[16] Regardless, this was the first time two teams from the same city would reach the final of the two major European competitions in the same season. However, as previously stated, the aim isn't to provide you with a history lesson, it's to use the historical perspective to sharpen our vision of the present.

To this extent there are many notable factors. Among them is that Stevie Chalmers scored the winning goal for Celtic in the 1967 final, and yet at the age of 23 was still playing in the 'juniors' for Ashfield Football Club. Alex James of Arsenal won the football league in 1931, 1933, 1934 and 1935, and the FA Cup in 1930 and 1936. James has been described as a genius with the ball at his feet, and Arsenal's first bona fide icon, the first player of his generation to be considered an 'artiste'.[17,18] The Arsenal official website describes James as 'one of the finest players to grace a football pitch and arguably the Dennis Bergkamp of his day. Alex James was a star of his time and a pivotal figure in Arsenal's domination of the 1930s.'

Notably, at the age of 20, James was still playing junior football before signing with Raith Rovers ahead of the 1922/23 season. At 5ft 6in, he had at first struggled to succeed because of his diminutive size.[19] He scored two of the goals in the 'Wembley Wizards' 5 -1 victory over England in 1928. Of the forwards who started that match, alongside James were Alex Jackson, James Dunn, Hughie Gallacher and Alan Morton. Out of the five of them, Jackson was the tallest at just 5ft 7in.[20] Like James and Stevie Chalmers, these players had all entered senior football at an older age than would be possible today.

Hughie Gallacher, James's great friend, would not only go on to be arguably Newcastle United's greatest-ever striker (scoring 143 goals in just 174 matches), but some consider him to one of the game's greatest centre-forwards of all time. Standing at 5ft 5in tall, Gallacher's skill, guile and instinct more than made up for what he lacked in natural physique.[21] As youngsters, both Gallacher and James were rejected by local team Bellshill Athletic for being 'far too small'. Instead, they were allowed to push the club hamper to and from the station for away matches and got paid half a crown for their efforts.[22]

If the players mentioned above, and countless more, had to come through today's system, then it's more than likely we would never have heard of them. The Scottish Football Hall of Fame would be unrecognisable, and we would be telling a very different historical story. Quite simply, today's System 1 isn't set up in the best way to allow these players the development time or entry point into professional football, let alone to go on to become legends of the game.

From a historical perspective, it was more than just the Old Firm, or England's best club teams that were full of good Scottish players. Players capable of mixing it with the best in Europe were everywhere. In keeping with the 'Vision' for Scottish football, stated earlier as 'a country where our best club teams regularly make it through the group stages of European competitions and can compete in the later stages'. One where 'the clubs below our top teams are also a hotbed of talented and technical players, ready and able to take a step up', the 20th century was a hotbed of technical and talented players, and it was distributed across more than today's two big clubs.

Dunfermline reached the quarter-finals of the Cup Winners' Cup in 1962 and the semi-finals in 1969. In between times they reached the quarter-finals of the Fairs

Cup in 1966. In the same tournament the following year Dundee United beat Barcelona home and away. In the next round, despite getting knocked out, they inflicted one of only six defeats that Italian giants Juventus would experience in all competition in 1966/67.[23] In the 1986/87 UEFA Cup, United would once again beat Barcelona home and away. After beating the Spanish giants 1-0 at Tannadice in the first leg, they went to Camp Nou two weeks later and won 2-1.[24]

It was United's neighbours, however, who nearly pulled off what would have been one of the biggest European results of the 60s. After winning the Scottish League in 1962, Dundee were Scotland's representatives in the 1962/63 European Cup. They reached the semi-finals and, despite winning the second leg 1-0, the damage had been done in the first leg. In front of 73,933 fans in the San Siro, Dundee went into half-time with the scores level at 1-1. Early in the second half, 20-year-old midfielder Doug Houston was through on goal but shot narrowly wide. Two quickfire but controversial goals followed, before two more concessions late on made AC Milan's trip to Dens Park something of a formality.[25]

Elsewhere, Kilmarnock managed a 2-2 draw at home to Real Madrid in the 1966 European Cup. The following year they reached the semi-finals of the Fairs Cup, where they were defeated by Don Revie's Leeds United. Leeds went down to Dinamo Zagreb in the final, in which, across the two legs, four Scots played for them: Willie Bell, Billy Bremner, Peter Lorimer and Eddie Gray.[26] Not surprisingly there was a belief, based on evidence, that Scottish players had what it took to play at the highest level.

Nowhere was this optimism more manifest than when Scotland reached then played in the 1974 World Cup finals in the then West Germany. In the lead-up to the tournament Scotland had qualified with a match to spare. Victories home and away against Denmark set up a showdown with Czechoslovakia at Hampden. The visitors took the early advantage, but that was cancelled out by Manchester United centre-back 'Big' Jim Holton, before Joe Jordan headed what would be the winning goal in the 74th minute. Scotland were on their way to their first appearance at the finals since 1958.

In the lead-up to the finals, optimism grew further with good performances on the park. This included victories over Norway and Wales, a draw against West Germany and a 2-0 win against England that started a run of three out of four victories against the Auld Enemy. There was a confidence to being Scottish and a professional footballer, perfectly summed up by the then Manchester United winger Willie Morgan: 'We felt we were one of the best teams in the world at the time and were capable of winning the World Cup.' According to Morgan, such was the confidence in the squad that they expected to beat Brazil in the second group match. Similarly, Morgan's team-mate, the Leeds United legend Peter Lorimer, felt that 'the belief in the squad and the quality in the squad was good enough to win the World Cup'.[27] It was a squad full of Scottish footballing legends that included Danny McGrain, Billy Bremner, Kenny Dalglish and Denis Law.[28]

Such was the abundance of talent available to Scotland at the time that notable players such as Pat Stanton, Bobby Lennox and Archie Gemmill didn't make the squad, while Jimmy Johnstone did but didn't play in any of the three matches.

An opening victory against Zaire was followed by a draw against Brazil, leaving Scotland needing to beat Yugoslavia to progress to the group stages. A draw was all Scotland could muster and they went out of the tournament, becoming the first team to go undefeated at the finals and not win the tournament.[29] Despite this disappointment, Scotland returned home as national heroes and went on to the qualify for the next four World Cup finals.

Scotland's reputation and prominence showed no sign of letting up. When it comes to the 'gaffers', all in all, six Scottish managers – Alex Ferguson, Jock Stein, Matt Busby, Willie Waddell, Bill Shankly and George Graham – have won 12 European trophies. The 1983 Cup Winners' Cup victory would only be the start of what was to come for Ferguson, who would go on to win six more European trophies. As it stands, only Carlo Ancelotti has won more than Ferguson.[30]

On the pitch, throughout the 70s and early 80s several Scottish players were among the most decorated players in Europe. Nowhere can this be seen more clearly than in the 22 players of the Scotland squad that contested the 1982 World Cup finals in Spain.[31] By the time they retired, they could boast 31 European club competition winners' medals between them (including UEFA Super Cups). In that squad were the likes of Kenny Dalglish, Graeme Souness and Alan Hansen – all multiple European competition winners with Liverpool FC – Alan Brazil, twice a UEFA Cup winner, and John Robertson, who won back-to-back European Cups with Nottingham Forest in 1979 and 1980.

Then we have the Aberdeen contingent of Jim Leighton, Willie Miller and Alex McLeish, who won the 1983 Cup Winners' Cup against Real Madrid in Gothenburg.

A further nine players from that squad would also finish their careers with at least one European club competition winners' medal. All in all, 14 players from the 22-man squad were European winners. Of those who didn't finish their careers with winners' medals, several came close. Joe Jordan would lose the 1973 Cup Winners' Cup Final and the 1975 European Cup Final with Leeds United. Paul Sturrock and David Narey lost the 1987 UEFA Cup Final with Dundee United. Three years earlier the pair had reached the semi-finals of the European Cup with United, eventually going down 3-2 on aggregate against AS Roma. In the other semi-final that year Liverpool defeated, Dinamo Bucharest. Remarkably of the 64 players (16 per team) who made up the first-team squads of the four teams in the semi-finals that year – 21 of them were Scottish – 16 of them played for United and five for Liverpool.

Then, what felt like almost overnight, largely speaking it all just stops! On the way to the UEFA Cup Final in 1987, as well as beating Barcelona home and away, Dundee United went to Germany and beat Borussia Mönchengladbach 2-0 to progress to the final. Since then they haven't been beyond the second round of any European competition. Aberdeen, following their night of triumph in 1983, followed this up with a semi-final appearance in the same tournament the next year. A quarter-final defeat to IFK Göteborg in the 1986 European Cup ended their brief adventure at the top table of European football. In the years that followed, the Dons have managed one appearance beyond the second round of European competition, going down 7-3 on aggregate to Bayern Munich in the third round of the 2007/08 UEFA Cup.

Celtic, from 1967-1974, competed in two finals, two semi-finals and three quarter-finals of the European Cup. In 1979/80 they narrowly lost to Real Madrid 3-2 in the quarter-finals of the premier cup; however, from then until the turn of the century, in all competitions in Europe they would progress beyond the second round on one occasion. On this occasion they were knocked out in the third round of the European Cup by Nottingham Forest. Rangers would famously win the Cup Winners' Cup in 1972 when they beat Dynamo Moscow in the Camp Nou. However, their most notable European campaign between the victory in Barcelona and the turn of the century would come in the 1992/93 Champions League. Their second-place finish in the group made them one of the top four teams in the tournament. Notably, 17 out of the 23-man Champions League squad that year were eligible to play for Scotland.[32]

In the 21st century, the lights have briefly flickered on and off again. A resurgent Celtic under Martin O'Neill reached the 2003 UEFA Cup Final in Seville, only to lose in extra time to Jose Mourinho's Porto. Then it was the turn of Rangers, who lost the 2008 final to a Zenit Saint Petersburg under their ex-manager Dick Advocaat. More recently, Rangers lost the 2022 UEFA Cup to Eintracht Frankfurt. Outside of this, from 1987 to the present, Scotland's impact on European football has largely disappeared. From the swagger and confidence of the 60s and 70s that bled in to the historic 80s, to a nation where it's quite literally anyone's guess what's going to happen when our clubs play in Europe.

This decline coincided with Scotland's fortunes on the pitch starting to show signs of concern. In 1990, Scotland competed in their fifth consecutive World Cup finals. In the first match they went down 1-0 to Costa Rica, before beating Sweden in match two. A defeat to Brazil in the final match sent Scotland home. Failure to qualify for the 1994 finals in the United States seemed to be a temporary blip, as Scotland once again qualified for the 1998 finals in France. As we now know, participation at the 1998 World Cup covered over the cracks of the later part of a century that for the most part had much to be proud of. We just didn't know it yet, but the cracks were going to get deeper and, so far, we haven't been able to fix them.

Reflections – undersized and overlooked versus 'the achterbankgeneratie'

The 20th century provides us with an insight into the quality and quantity of Scottish players who made it so memorable. The potted history outlined only scratches the surface of the story. There are many omissions, both in the players who could have featured but didn't and the stories that could have been told but weren't. When you reach a saturation point with your findings then that's a good place to stop. This happens in research when the same themes keep recurring. When themes start to develop, it gives us the information we need to start to make comparisons and help us better understand the areas we're investigating. In this case comparisons between the past and the present for the purposes of thinking about addressing them for a better future.

The 20th century, then, has two major themes of interest that shine a light on where both society and the nature of the game has changed today. The first theme has already been discussed – football was a way out of social and cultural hardship for many in the Scotland of the 20th century. The developmental experiences of Scottish players throughout the century adds weight to what's called the 'talent needs trauma' theory.[33] It's now widely accepted that the development of exceptional talent isn't a steady and smooth process. Instead, it's what researchers have come to characterise as the 'rocky road to the top' that allows an individual to accrue the mental toughness and resilience needed to succeed.[34]

There are, for most, significantly fewer challenges inherent in the life of youngsters in today's Scotland. The set-up of elite academy systems has led to concerns that it drives sport towards the middle classes, and with this the nature in which children are parented and experience sport. Annette Lareau's social research has observed that upper- and middle-class parents try to develop their children's talents in a concerted fashion.[35] According to Lareau, 'Organized activities, established and controlled by mothers and fathers, dominate the lives of middle-class children. By making certain their children have these and other experiences, middle-class parents engage in a process of concerted cultivation.' In contrast to this, Lareau argues that working-class and poor families view it as a positive outcome if a child's natural growth has been sustained. To this extent, working-class parents and poorer parents have a different cultural approach, where growth is more natural and organic rather than directed and managed.

Organic growth contrasts with what Dutch psychologist Jan Derksen describes as 'the achterbankgeneratie' (backseat generation). This refers to the generation of children growing up in the backseat of their parents' car as they're driven to and from extracurricular activity.[36] This has been characterised as 'helicopter parenting' or 'snowplough parenting' in which parents act as helicopters hovering above children, overseeing their every move, or snowploughs to smooth the way for their development. While no one would argue for a return to the social conditions of the early to mid-20th century, from a talent development perspective, we need to look at how we can deliberately build in desirable difficulties in the progression of a young player. Especially as the characteristics needed to succeed are strongly associated with struggle and of overcoming challenges.

The second theme that characterised the system of the 20th century is that the pathway into professional football of that century, by today's standards, was a late-entry system. Stevie Chalmers was playing with the juniors at 23 and then went on to score the winning goal in the European Cup Final. For the numerous physically diminutive players, such as James and Gallacher, the late-entry system gave them the time needed to close the physical gap. In theory, this meant that by the time they caught up physically, their superior technical skills would come to the fore. As such, we need to consider that a system that doesn't cater as well for 'physical' development time inadvertently may be shutting out the more gifted individuals. They in turn are in danger of being lost to the game and to the nation.

The end of the century, in player development terms, is also notable for two major factors at a government and footballing level. Firstly, Scotland's demise as a production line for talent can be traced back to the Bosman ruling that allowed out-of-contract players over the age of 23 to move freely within the European Community. The ruling was the outcome of a long and protracted dispute between Jean-Marc Bosman and RFC Liège, involving his refusal to sign a much-reduced one-year contract.

However, it was a decision not long after that would change the face of football as we knew it. On 19 February 1996, UEFA abolished what was known as the 3+2 rule that applied to its European club competitions.[37] The rule meant that a club could field three foreign players, plus two more if they had come through the club's academy system. In Scotland the effect of the Bosman ruling created a sea change in the way clubs thought about fielding the strongest team possible. According to Fraser Wishart, the current chief executive of the Scottish Professional Footballers' Association, 'The thinking among Scottish clubs was "why should we bother rearing our own players if we can't cash in on them?" Instead, clubs signed what they thought was the finished article from abroad.'[38]

Around the same time, a second change was being ushered in under the name of the 'Scottish Youth Football Initiative' – a partnership between the SFA, the SPL and the SFL.[39] This would be the forerunner to what's now known as the pro-youth system. This saw a more structured and controlled approach to player development. Then, in 1999, and perhaps as the full force of the Bosman was starting to be felt, the seeds were being planted that would see the introduction of the UEFA Club Licensing System.

At the time, there were common concerns about inadequate governance structures, poor infrastructure, unsatisfactory financial planning and, most significantly for this discussion, a lack of youth investment.[40] Club licensing was deemed to be the appropriate tool to address these issues. Scotland was part of the pilot project in 2001 and one of the first nations to be awarded the new licence in 2004. Significantly, for a club to meet the youth development criteria, they must meet Article 20, which states that the licence applicant must have the following youth teams within its legal entity: at least four youth teams within the age range of 10 to 21; at least one U10 team or organised football activities for U10s.[41]

The seeds of System 1 were now firmly in place and, as we'll come to see, the seeds haven't flourished as we hoped they would. The end of the century, the UEFA Club Licensing System and the player pathway issues created by the Bosman ruling will come to dominate much of the discussions on what has become of player development in the first quarter of the 21st century. For the moment it's worth reflecting that these changes would have a significant effect on the elite system, as it now pushes the age of first selection down to a much younger age. While 'the Scottish Football Initiative' of 1995 was originally set up for 14–15-year-olds, the UEFA scheme would push things down to the U10 age range, and now things are going to get more problematic, particularly if you're the next Alex James, Stevie Chalmers or hundreds of others we could choose from the 20th century!

Chapter 3

Environment, identity and managers

BEFORE MOVING into the matters of the 21st century, this chapter brings the first section of the book to a close with some reflections on the two previous centuries. From a historical perspective, what seems to connect much of the story so far is that of our strong 'identity' of being good at football and of the environment that shaped both the psyche and skills of the Scottish player. I was genuinely struck by the conviction with which we believed we could win the World Cup in 1974. Willie Morgan genuinely believed this, as did Peter Lorimer and many others. And why not! If your team is strong enough to leave out Pat Stanton, Bobby Lennox and Archie Gemmill, then you know you must be good, and so must your team-mates.

However, you need more than to just know you're good – perhaps even world-class (we'll come to that!). As such, this chapter looks at this in more detail and the factors I feel we should pay attention to, particularly in relation to how this psyche and identity was developed, and how it aligns with some ideas from the psychological sciences.

Environment

Whenever I start a conversation on the role of the environment in player development, I always begin by trying to impress that when we interact with an environment and the conditions in it for long enough, we're changed by the experience. I highlight this because it's not through choice – it's a function of life! Hence the well-used saying that 'you're a product of your environment'. Some even say we grow up to be the average of the six people we spend most time with. There are many contributing factors, such as where you grow up, who your parents are, your early life experiences, your friends, your first coach in sport, your siblings, your outlook on life – they all play a part. There's example after example of the conditions of our upbringing being fundamental to who we are and what we become. When it comes to getting good at anything it's no different – how you train, where you train, who you train with and how often you train really matters!

What then of the environmental conditions of growing up in Scotland and being into football? For hundreds of Scottish professional players it was the streets and any other available spaces. One such space would be the 'dreaded' red-ash pitches made from burnt colliery waste. For most it wouldn't have dawned on them that these environmental conditions would be a key factor in the development of their footballing skills and attributes. From the mid-50s onwards, particularly in the west of Scotland, every primary school and secondary school had one, some areas had multiple. Just off Shieldhall Road in Drumoyne (formerly part of the Burgh of Govan) they famously had 50 red-ash pitches and would provide the setting for many a professional player's formative years. The ball was even worse. The rough gravelly surface would destroy a leather ball so Mitre brought out the infamous Mouldmaster ball, a hard, dimply, netball-type sphere that was the least enjoyable thing you could ever kick. A mistimed chip, long pass or shot could leave you writhing in agony. As such it lent itself to being passed along the ground, dribbled with or scooped/flicked through the air – the likes of which Jim Baxter indulged in just after his keepie-uppies on the Wembley pitch in 1967.

As for street football, many consider it to be one of the main factors that produced so many great Scottish football players. Why kids stopped playing football in the street isn't exactly known – too many cars, too many dangers, video games, the media – perhaps a combination of factors. What does seem to be clear is that when the 'streets closed' Scotland's greatest talent development system closed too. Street football, of course, wasn't confined to the street, it could break out anywhere, if not on the street then in a yard, the park, the beach, your mate's back garden, the school playground – any available space. Street football wasn't necessarily about playing in the street, it was more to do with its implicit conventions; it was, in fact, any form of football that shared the same defining features: no written rules, no limit on playing area, no limit on number of players, no officials/adults, no time limit on matches, no age limits, and matches would typically finish when whoever owned the ball got fed up or had to go home.

More to the point, and relevant to this discussion, is what was it about the red-ash pitches and street football that provided so much by way of the conditions required to be good at football? We've come to know these environments as 'self-organised' learning systems. This means that, rather than being taught what to do, the environment is the teacher, as it implies what needs to be learned. A sense of survival is implied, and this requires an individual to acquire an array of skills, guile and physical qualities. Survival could mean avoiding injury because of the playing surfaces, developing the upper-body strength to stay on your feet, or the speed of thought to counteract a mismatch in physicality – this involves a sense of your own strengths and weaknesses as well as those of your opponents.

All these learning opportunities were inherent in the conditions of many Scots' upbringings. The surface of the red-ash pitch taught you to stay on your feet, to balance, to be aware of not only other players but other hazards. They rutted in the cold or when it got wet, and rocks and broken glass weren't uncommon on the pitch. As one Scottish journalist put it:

> The red ash pitches were the scene of nightmares for many a young whippersnapper who felt like they needed an arm or leg transplant after coming into contact with the surface at speed … and then there was the added, unspeakable, torture of taking a bath after a game, the pitch having the macabre quality of being able to hurt you even when you weren't on it.[1]

Willie Miller, the Aberdeen legend, describes playing most of his youth football on Glasgow Green and its collection of red-ash pitches. Miller doesn't romanticise about the experience, describing them as evil concoctions and vicious, but does concede that they enhanced his ability to balance and had made him physically stronger. He was also hit by a stolen car while playing street football.[2] The street had a sense of chaos to it, with uneven playing surfaces. Spectators and players could merge into one, no strips, and many other external sources of information challenging you beyond simply playing the game. And play the game we did! In the absence of adult involvement and other distractions of modern-day life, the street, beach, red-ash or school playground stimulated the interest of children to such an extent that the vast number of practice hours needed to become good at an activity were easily accumulated by a young age.

What we see here is that the conditions of the learning environment are tougher than the real game. Not only did you have to contend with many 'external' distractions, in those days you had to risk serious injury to play the game you loved. When this happens, the real game can seem easier. You in effect train beyond the needs of the activity. These training conditions are strongly associated with the performance psychology phenomenon known as the 'flow' state. Several studies have shown that it's likely that individuals with higher ability have higher flow values.[3] In many ways this state has come to characterise those who can perform when it really matters, who don't fold under pressure, who always turn up on the big occasions.[4] When practice is more difficult than the real game, an individual enters a state of 'flow' because they perceive their abilities to be equal to or greater than the task in hand.

Flow then can't be achieved when a training activity is continuously stopped and started again. Or indeed when the game is broken down in training to such an extent that it's unrecognisable to the real game. Such activities are associated with drills that are accompanied with high volumes of instruction. In this situation there's a danger that the opposite becomes true. The individual is now training below the needs of the activity and is likely to have a completely different perception of their skills relative to the challenges of the real game. One thing for sure when we look at the highly structured nature of kids' coaching today is this: no child with an open space to play in and in possession of a ball has ever asked for some cones so they could set up a training drill. If you give kids a football and an open space a match will break out and, to the greatest extent possible, it will look and feel like the real thing.

Furthermore, consider the developmental environment of players in elite academies today. For most, the developmental environment is one of 4G Astro pitches and little distraction. Perfect conditions don't make skilful footballers. It's worth noting that these aren't just the conditions of the elite system in Scotland, these are the same conditions you're likely to find in any academy system the world over. There are other factors at play that are more unique to Scotland, which we'll come to talk about later, that when added to the 'mix' have loaded the probability of us producing top players against us.

I've found countless examples of 'difficulties' in the environment during my time researching talent development, particularly in the developmental backgrounds of world-class performers and those who most exhibit the characteristic of being in a state of flow. For example, and like many Scots, for Johan Cruyff everything started on

80

the street. Cruyff grew up in Betondorp, a village built in the 1920s as a housing project experiment in using cheap materials, the name literally translating as the concrete village. It's perhaps hard to imagine the landscape of such an environment. To paint the picture, developments such as these have come to be known as 'brutalist' architecture for the blocky angular look and the large-scale use of poured concrete.

In a passage from Cruyff's autobiography he talks about his upbringing and where he learned his skills:

> It was working class, and as kids we spent as much time out of the house as possible; from as early as I can remember we played football everywhere we could. It was here I learned to think about how to turn a disadvantage into an advantage. You see that the kerb isn't actually an obstacle, but that you can turn it into a teammate for a one–two. So, thanks to the kerb I was able to work on my technique. When the ball bounces off different surfaces at odd angles, you have to adjust in an instant.[5]

Cruyff credits the *concrete village* for honing his exceptional skills. The angular nature of the environment for his unique passing vision and his dislike of falling on concrete is credited for his superior balance and ability to react to unpredictable situations. He would advocate that young players trained in flat soles because studs made it too easy to balance. The nature of Cruyff's story is one of skill emerging out of the conditions in the environment. His story is a common one that repeats itself time and time again when you go looking for the genesis of skilful, creative, surprising, awe-inspiring performances.

From football to art, from skateboarding to music, from architecture to poetry. The powerful influence of the environment from a skill development point of view is nicely brought to life in the case of Rodney Mullen. The godfather of street skateboarding, Mullen is credited with inventing numerous tricks, including the ollie, kickflip and the 360-flip. When Mullen runs out of ideas for a new trick or move, he simply finds a new environment, with a new set of problems in it, and sets about playing with the conditions in his new environment.[6]

Returning to football, for Socrates, the Brazilian footballer, environmental problems were a key factor in the development of his playing ability:

> We started playing football on the street with an avocado seed ... the fact that I had learned this way was excellent. When you play in an orchard, with irregular surfaces and surrounded by trees, there is a need for developing a bunch of abilities in order to prevent injuries. To not get hurt, and to your eye on [...] the ball and on the game, we also needed to keep an eye out for the mango trees and their roots on the ground.[7]

Many Brazilian players of the past have described that the conditions of the real game were easier than the environmental conditions of the matches they played growing up. Playing at the World Cup on perfectly manicured pitches, with a perfect football and the wide-open spaces of a full-sized pitch felt too easy. These conditions were in stark contrast to the *pelada* (naked) form of the game they played as youngsters, where often barefooted matches were played on the street, beach, court, dirt-fields – different surfaces and conditions that generated different variations of football matches.

To illustrate the powerful role the environment plays in player development further, I've posed this thought experiment often at talks on the role of the environment on the development of performance:

> If Lionel Messi had left the Hospital Italiano on 24 June 1987 and, instead of heading for the La Bajada neighbourhood of Rosario[8] (186 miles north-west of Buenos Aires), he moved to live with an adopted family somewhere in the Scottish Highlands, does he still grow up to be (arguably) the world's greatest-ever footballer?

The answer to this question will reveal much about your beliefs regarding the nature of talent. If you answered yes, then why do believe this? Likewise, if no, then why? Here's my thinking: I don't think he does, or at least the odds are stacked strongly against him. The probability is stronger that by this stage in his life he's playing shinty and on the verge of breaking the legendary Kingussie Camanachd forward Robert Ross's record of being the only player to score more than 1,000 goals in the sport. For many, Ross is the greatest player to ever wield a caman, and is known as 'reliable winner, technically gifted genius and the relentless trainer'. His nickname, somewhat ironically, is 'The Ronaldo of the Glens'![9]

It's unlikely that there's a 'gene' coded into your DNA for being good at football, shinty or anything else for that matter. What we do know, however, without fear of contradiction, is that if you change the mix, you change the outcome!

To that extent, if, on the other hand, Messi had been born in the 20s, 30s or 40s in the Ayrshire village of Glenbuck, then the chances are he does grow up to be a footballing great. All that remains today in Glenbuck is a granite memorial to the great Bill Shankly, a memorial that's more than just a tribute to a footballing great, it's a reminder of a place that was known as the 'village of football', which, according to the authors of *Shankly's Village*, although never exceeding a population of 1,700, produced more than 50 professional footballers over a 40-year period – proportionality akin to a non-league team in London producing 250,000 players over the same timescale.[10] Not unsurprisingly, Messi's actual birthplace, Rosario, is known as the 'cradle of football' because of the volume of great players (and managers) that have emerged from the small port city.

Whichever way you look at it, the conditions in our environment shape who we become. This is both a threat and an opportunity for those working in TID – particularly heads of performance and the coaches who work underneath them. The environment of our player development system has the power to lift us to new heights, but it can also crush us. A good young player in the wrong environment will struggle to progress. A perceived lesser player in a good environment has more chance. The role of the environment has played out strongly in the story so far. The rocky road to success of the conditions of our upbringing and early footballing experience, to the 'snowplough' parenting of the present, who try to smooth the bumps in the way to stardom; the Bosman ruling; the UEFA licensing criteria – all represent 'changes' to the mix that have changed the 'outcome' on the pitch.

Identity (crisis)

The prominence in the game established by Scottish players at the end of the 19th century had carried into the 20th century, gained momentum and fuelled the many great players and achievements previously mentioned. If any one single characteristic prevailed throughout the 19th century and the best part of the 20th that doesn't seem to be evident today, it's a confidence on the pitch from the inner belief in your own abilities and those of your team-mates and of believing you're better than your opponent. When it comes to the matter of identity, and this inner belief, the word that keeps reappearing in the folklore of Scottish football and seems to best describe our identity on the pitch is the word *gallus* – or the term 'gallus Scots'!

The term itself is a colloquialism most used in the west of Scotland to describe behaviour or actions that can be unmanageable, bold, daring, impish, mischievous, cheeky. The origin of the word is less clear, some saying that historically someone acting in a gallus manner is usually doing something wrong, and as such is fit to be hung from the gallows.[11] I'm not convinced by that interpretation. Instead, I prefer the one drawn from the Latin word *gallus*, which means rooster, and the use of the term seems to have some origin in cockfighting. It's said that the cock pit is where the character of the rooster is wagered on, a place where the rooster can show grit and gameness and display evidence of its courage. It's noteworthy that if a rooster runs or declines to fight it's said to have turned 'chicken'[12] It evokes the notion of the bird of good character strutting around the pen with its chest puffed out. It seems to fit. I like the thought that the Scots marauded across the pitch with their chests puffed out and a brand of football that was bold and daring.

How the term gallus arrived in the west of Scotland, and who gave us the label, is anyone's guess. What's certain is that it was applied to characterise the identity of the Scottish player. Identity matters, all great footballing nations have an identity, and while this doesn't characterise every player, it's the qualities you think of when you think of them. Identity gives direction to our actions and our mentality. Something for those coming up to aspire to. Something to want to emulate and be like. However, like Scotland, the loss of identity is most talked about when teams are struggling to emulate former glories.

For example, Brazil is known for the *'ginga'* style that characterises a sway-like flow to their movement patterns. Identity, much like the gallus Scots, is influenced at a cultural level. *Ginga* was influenced by the martial art called capoeira and the principles of samba dance. *Ginga* came to characterise the Brazilian style and is connected to their expression of *malandragem* (i.e. cunning). Much like our lineage to the Scotch Professors, the cultural emergence of *malandragem* dates to the 19th century and the abolition of the slave trade. Many individuals couldn't obtain regular work and became street figures who had to live on their wits and charms, so they developed street smarts and cunning to survive.[13]

Malandragem, underpinned by *ginga*, was first alluded to as a football concept by the Brazilian social historian Gilberto Freyre, who lauded the distinctively expressive, creative and individualistic qualities of Brazilian players during the 1938 World Cup:

> Our football style seems to contrast with the European one due to an amount of qualities such as surprise, skill, cleverness, speed and, at the same time, individual brilliance and spontaneity [...] Our passes, our catches, our misleads, our floridness with the ball ... there is something that reminds one of dancing and capoeira, making the Brazilian way of playing football a trademark, which sophisticates and often sweetens the game invented by the English and played so stiffly by them.[14]

The lineage and timeline expressed by Freyre has a cultural connection to British football. It wasn't until the mulattos (an outdated term used to describe people of mixed African and European ancestry) and black players were incorporated into the teams formed by white elite football 'founders' that the concept of *ginga* emerged. Like the gallus Scot of yesterday this identity and style is seldom seen today. When it comes to thinking of the modern-day Brazilian *malandros* (the adjective of *malandragem*) type of player who uses a *ginga* style, one thinks of Ronaldinho or more recently of Neymar Jnr.[15] However, these players are now few and far between, to such an extent that Pelé called for a return to the *ginga* style in the aftermath of Brazil's exit from the 2014 World Cup, and the 2015 Copa America quarter-final defeat to Paraguay.[16]

In 2017, Paolo Maldini lamented the fading identity and reputation of Italian football. An Italian team last won the Champions League in the 2009/10 season and, as a nation, the World Cup in 2006. According to Maldini, 'Italian football needs to start over again, as a country we are searching for an identity.'[17] For Italy that identity was less about the individual characteristics of the Brazilian *malandros* and more about a collective mindset associated with their defensive style of play. If Brazil's identity was rooted in the belief that the objective of the game was to score more than the opponent, then you might say the Italian mindset was to concede one fewer. Characterised as *catenaccio*, the system was pioneered by Servette coach Karl Rappan in the 1930s. Servette, a semi-professional club, struggled when they came up against physically stronger professional teams who routinely adopted the 2-3-5 system. He developed a tactic that allowed his teams to absorb pressure before hitting on the counter-attack. To do so he pulled his two wing-halves back to essentially form a back four, three of whom were fixed in a man-marking role, leaving one as an attacking centre-back to act as playmaker. This essentially created the modern 4-4-2 system.[18]

Its greatest exponents became Helenio Herrera's Internazionale. In 1967, Herrera's *catenaccio* style met a group of gallus Scots in the European Cup Final. On this occasion the Scots, chests puffed out, demonstrated that the best way to overcome mass defence was to engage in mass attack.[19] On display that night was McIlvanney's characterisation of the Scots' identity, that of a collective self-assurance, a refusal to be belittled or taken for granted. So reviled was the *catenaccio* style in Britain that the Scots' triumph over this negative system is said to have been the inspiration for Bill Shankly's famous words to Jock Stein that he was 'immortal now'.

When it comes to thinking of our identity today and of players strutting about the pitch, chests puffed out, making their mark at the highest level, a question that often gets asked is: who was Scotland's last world-class player? At least I often ask it! This is, of course, a tricky question, the first problem being that before you even get to the question, you need agreement on the definition of world-class. Then, naturally you must go back several decades and beyond to identify players who would even be good enough to form part of the argument. Kenny Dalglish? Definitely! Paul McStay and Barry Ferguson, world-class? Not for me, but could have been, perhaps? Davie Cooper? Again, maybe yes, maybe no! It's a question that could fill many an hour of a Saturday radio show or phone-in. Not only is world-class hard to define from a technical point of view, but it also has a large circumstantial element to it. Dalglish played in a world-class team at Liverpool surrounded by world-class team-mates. Perhaps if McStay, Ferguson, Cooper and many others had too, then their status would also have been elevated. Luck, opportunity and timing all play a part. Before Jock Stein assembled his world-class team, many of the players wouldn't have been considered as such. As with all matters Scottish football, we might need to agree to disagree! Perhaps a better question is: who were Scotland's last gallus players? Now, it's possible to be gallus and not a great footballer, but is it possible to be a great player and not gallus?

On the question of who our last gallus player was, step forward James McFadden. McFadden will be forever remembered for the 35-yard screamer he hit past the French keeper to win the match for Scotland against France in Paris in 2007. One of those iconic goals in the 'dark blue' strip that's up there in my memory with the likes of David Narey's strike against Brazil in the 1982 World Cup finals, Kenny Dalglish's Euro qualifier goal against Belgium in 1982 or, more recently, the two free kicks Leigh Griffiths scored against England in 2017. Many will also remember McFadden's goal against Macedonia at Hampden in 2009, dribbling from his own half before rounding the keeper and rolling the ball into an empty net.

Notably, these goals came as no surprise to those watching who had come to associate McFadden with these types of exploits during his career. McFadden, speaking on the *Open Goal* podcast, describes himself as the 'the wee gallus boy from the scheme'.[20] Fortunately for McFadden, after coming off the streets and into Motherwell's professional pathway, it was a positive encounter with a coach that let that gallus streak come to the fore: 'When I was playing in the U14/15 ... the big boy Paul Smith kind of accepted that's the way I was, the wee gallus boy from the scheme ... I didn't take any rubbish and [...] he accepted that and kind of just let me express myself.' McFadden credits the conditions of his upbringing for developing his qualities as a player, that of a working-class background, red-ash pitches and playing in the streets of Springburn for hours on end.

What's clear it that McFadden not only exhibited the characteristics of the gallus Scot, but he also displayed the previously mentioned positive attributes of being able to access a flow-like state. He, like so few in this day and age, was able to perform and do special things on the biggest stage. This is associated with the type of activities you're exposed to and the extent that it equips you with skills that equal the occasion. You can't teach skill, but you can give it the conditions to flourish.

Not surprisingly, McFadden has some concerns about the way players are coached and how this may be limiting the development of players with something that 'wee bit different'. In this sense, it may be that we don't need to coach kids how to be gallus but instead we need to make sure we don't 'coach it out of them'! We need to engage in activities where they experience flow and are connected to team-mates who are simultaneously experiencing the same thing, the type of mentality that makes you believe you can win the World Cup, and one that makes you disappointed when you only draw with Brazil.

You'll have experienced a flow-like state yourself. It's associated with a feeling of a loss of time, where thinking is overcome by doing, when you're immersed in an activity. When the light faded on the street game and you were told it was time to go home. On these occasions you were in a flow-like state and you were developing skills, even though you didn't know it.

Youth identity

When it comes to the issue of 'youth identity' the modern and generally accepted characterisation of 'youth' is credited to the pioneering American psychologist G. Stanley Hall from as far back as 1904.[21] Hall introduced the notion that adolescence is a period of 'storm and stress', of conflicts and mood swings and an enthusiasm for risky behaviour. All characteristics that can be seen in abundance when youths congregate in groups, be it at the local 4G Astro pitch or on the streets of past decades and that are associated with the qualities of being gallus. However, the implementation of early entry to highly formalised and structured training activities requires children to leave this identity 'at the door'. Quite soon, play becomes work. When play stops and work begins it takes on a variant form of Max Weber's 'protestant work ethic' – the 'Scottish work ethic' – that emphasises hard work, sacrifice and education.[22] Here the identity of youth, perhaps for the first time, butts up against an ethic that dictates that those working hard should be selected for better positions, more responsibility and ultimately promotion. A sense of compliance, if you like. It has created a liking for terms such as 'hard work beats talent when talent fails to work hard', first coined by basketball coach Tim Notke and popularised by basketball legend Kevin Durant.[23]

It some respects it's used as a threat and a justification for a proclivity towards the virtues of hard work, the problem being the hard work over talent aphorism only has superficial merit, but it doesn't hold water when it comes to performing at an elite level. Its very notion is potentially damaging our production of better players, more technical, creative, irreverent ones. It warns you that you if you have talent and don't work hard, then your talent will be wasted. 'Wasted talent' has been levelled at many a high-profile Scottish player and it's most often the player with something a 'wee bit different'. It conjures up a Leigh Griffiths or a Derek Riordan type of player. The type of player who fans get excited about, who gets them off their feet, who does things on the park that will be long talked about.

It's said that you're experiencing an identity crisis when you've lost a sense of personal 'sameness' that's brought on by a loss of historical continuity.[24] Somewhere along the way, the bloodline to the gallus Scot, embedded within a like-minded group of team-mates, has been severed. A loss of identity has gone hand in hand with our downward spiral and status in the game. It would be difficult to describe to someone what our identity is today in the 21st century. It would for the best part conjure up a somewhat negative characterisation rather than a positive one. What's for sure is that we're currently experiencing an identity crisis in Scottish football.

An identity crisis doesn't need to be a terminal crisis. Instead it signals a turning point when development needs to move one way or the other. When it comes to addressing a loss of identity it's possible to embrace the old ways and adapt them to a new environment. While I'm old enough to remember my past and the identity of the gallus Scot, the term will mean little to those in the system today. We've already discussed the conditions with which this psyche might have emerged, the rocky road to success and the associated development of flow that suggest how we came to be gallus. We need to take the best parts of our culture and build on them to improve further on what was previously achieved. New knowledge and understanding when blended with our historical identity can be a potent mix, one where skill and belief in yourself and those around you creates an identity that you don't need to talk about – everyone can see it!

Bring in the experts

Before we move into the next century, it has perhaps been notable that there has been very little discussion on the great Scottish managers and coaches. Beyond talking about the social conditions and communities of their upbringing, I couldn't find the story from a historical perspective that would sharpen my vision on the present. That aside, the story of the greatest Scottish managers of all time sits clearly with the managers previously detailed, those who won European Cups and became legends of the game both at home and south of the border. However, there was an additional story that hasn't so far been mentioned and it has an interesting sub-plot to it that I think is worth highlighting. So, I will.

The last time Scotland qualified for the World Cup in 1990 and 1998, we had two former schoolteachers in charge. The first was Andy Roxburgh, who in his latter playing career was also headteacher at Carlibar Primary School in Barrhead.[25] Roxburgh moved into a Director of Coaching role with the SFA and was responsible for Scotland's only ever major triumph in international football when he guided Scotland's U18 team to a European Championship victory over Finland. His accomplishment of reaching two major finals would be celebrated widely today but perhaps this wasn't his greatest achievement. In 1993 he left his post as national manager to become UEFA's first technical director and institute the framework to raise the standard of coaching throughout Europe – today all 53 members are signed up to its principles. He's also responsible for the UEFA Grassroots charter based on the philosophy of 'No roots – no flowers – no future'.[26] It also shouldn't escape the attention that as early as 1991 Roxburgh was advocating the principles of a small-sided game approach to the development of players that the Belgians now credit for the emergence of so many technically gifted players.

Roxburgh would be replaced by Craig Brown, who towards the end of his career had trained in physical education and primary teaching at Jordanhill College before spending ten years as a primary school headteacher then as a lecturer in primary education while managing Clyde part-time. Prior to becoming the national manager, Brown, who on leaving Clyde had joined Scotland as assistant manager, notably oversaw Scotland's U16s to the final of the 1989 FIFA U16 World Championship before coaching the U21s to the semi-finals of the 1992 UEFA U21 Championship. Brown took the national men's team to the Euros and to the World Cup finals in France in 1998. Since Brown left his post in 2002 Scotland have been through seven managers and are now on their eighth. To this day, 25 years on, he's the last man to take Scotland to the World Cup finals.

When the SFA set up the first coaching education in 1957, it was the first in Europe to do this. They turned to Brown's father, who was the Director of the Scottish School of Physical Education at Jordanhill. After setting up the course, Brown Snr handed it over to Roy Small, the head of physical education at Jordanhill.[27] Brown and Roxburgh would go on to become paid-up members of what became known as the Largs mafia. For many in the Scottish public, Largs came to symbolise a closed shop, jobs for the boys type of mentality, but for those involved it was far from it. When Roxburgh took over from Small he gave the course a more international dimension, with the likes of Arrigo Sacchi, Rinus Michels and Marcello Lippi attending to distil their knowledge. It became so influential to Alex Ferguson that after his first visit he returned year on year for refresher courses. The list of high-profile coaches to pass through Largs is endless: Jose Mourinho, Andre Villas-Boas, and Fabio Cappello on an exchange trip arranged by the Italian FA watched Brown take a session. The notable individuals who passed through Largs goes some way to highlight the value they placed on receiving their coaching education in Scotland at the time.

This focus on education and the great managers in sport can't be ignored. Udo Lattek was pursuing a career as a teacher when, to the disbelief of many, he became the assistant coach to Helmut Schön at the 1966 World Cup. In 1970, on the advice of Franz Beckenbauer, Bayern Munich appointed Lattek as first-team coach. Lattek went on to win 15 major trophies while managing Bayern, Borussia Mönchengladbach and Barcelona, and is regarded as one of the game's all-time greats.[28] In the years since Lattek made the jump from education to the world of football coaching, notable individuals have done the same thing: Gérard Houllier, Jose Mourinho, Louis van Gaal, Rinus Michels, Guus Hiddink, plus the longest-serving manager in the Bundesliga, Christian Streich. Former All Blacks rugby coach Sir Graham Henry and former British Lions head coach Sir Ian McGeechan also trained as PE teachers, while Eddie Jones, the Australian former head coach of the England rugby team, studied PE at Sydney University before taking his first teaching job at the International Grammar School in the city's suburbs.[29]

When Michel Sablon, the then technical director of the Belgian FA, was tasked with turning around the fortunes of the Belgian national team, he turned to education for help. That help came in the form of the University of Louvain and Professor Werner Helsen. In 2006, Sablon presented his blueprint, *La vision de formation de l'URBSFA*, based on Helsen's recommendations.[30] Alongside Sablon during the Belgian football revolution were his colleagues Bob Browaeys and Jan Van Winckel, who both hold master's degrees in physical education. The result of the analysis would support the federation's theory of the importance of small-sided games, 2v2, 5v5 and 8v8 up until the U14 age group, to support the national team's philosophy of playing 4-3-3.[31]

At FC Barcelona Johan Cruyff and Pep Guardiola may be the names that are credited for the tactical evolution at FC Barcelona, but Professor Francisco (Paco) Seirul-lo is the constant that links these eras together. Seirul-lo started working with the Blaugrana in 1978 and, alongside the coach Joan Vilà, pioneered training methodologies that have impacted not only team sport but thinking in the movement of sciences, economics and telecommunications.[32]

While Roxburgh and Brown won't go down in Scottish football history for their accomplishments as players, like many of the names mentioned above their backgrounds were in more diverse but related fields of expertise. For these individuals their route to the top of their fields of coaching and management wasn't direct. To become a schoolteacher, you need an undergraduate degree before going on to study for a professional graduate diploma in education. This then qualifies you in the domains of expertise to work with young people.

Should the profession of coaching be any different? If you work as a coach, you work in the education industry. If you apply the principles of education to help people become better at sport, you're also working in the *movement sciences.* To study professionally in education and/ or the movements sciences involves an understanding of psychology, motor learning and physiology, to name just a few.

As we move into the 21st century, I'll leave the last word on this to César Luis Menotti, Argentina's World Cup-winning manager: 'Those who *only know about football, don't know about football.*'[33] In other words, the solution to the problem of systematically producing high-quality footballers, in a multimillion-pound industry, can't just be a football problem!

Section 2 – Present

Chapter 4

Review of 'the Review of Scottish Football' – Part 1: Talent, talent, talent

WE NOW reach the middle section of the book, which will act as a bridge between the past and the future. As we turn the page into a new period we leave behind a century that delivered so much on the pitch then faded out badly. The century ended with two major regulation changes that have changed the face of youth football: the influential Bosman ruling and the meeting of clubs, governing associations and UEFA in 1999 that led to the UEFA Club Licence that clubs need if they want to play in UEFA club competitions.

Most relevant to this discussion are Articles 19 and 20 from the regulations regarding the criteria for youth development. The SFA was part of the pilot programme and one of the first to gain a licence in 2004. Not long after, in May 2009, former First Minister of Scotland Henry McLeish was asked by the SFA to undertake a 'Review of Scottish Football' (the 'review').[1] The 'review' was to consider three key areas: 1) an extensive review of grassroots football and youth development, coupled with a review of the facilities and resources associated to this; 2) a critical analysis of how talent is nurtured and developed, with a view towards how other countries do it; 3) how the first two phases should shape the way in which the professional game is run.

In 2010, two reports, 'The Grassroots, Recreation and Youth Development' and 'Governance, Leadership and Structures' were published, the recommendations of which would be overwhelmingly implemented.[2] Alongside the implications of the Bosman ruling and the new UEFA Club Licensing System, we were soon going to undergo the most significant overhaul of the game, particularly in relation to youth development, that it had ever experienced.[3]

The aim of the next two chapters of the book is to look at the key aspects of the 'review', the arguments for change that were made in it and the thinking behind them. If the UEFA Club Licensing System forced our hand in relation to what a formalised youth development structure must include, the 'review' would be the driving force behind the finer detail. This finer detail would include much about our perception and treatment of 'talent', and the need to address the level of skill in Scottish players that the 'review' identified as being 'well below that of other comparable countries and Leagues' and what we need to do about it.

Talent, talent and talent!

If any concept, notion, idea or theory jumps off the pages of the 'review' more than any other, it's the regular references to and messages about the role of 'talent' in reviving our fortunes on the pitch. According to McLeish, to return to 'the golden age', a time of endless natural and indigenous talent, we need to address the talent 'gap' as this is where other countries have a competitive edge. As such, the notion of 'talent' has been placed 'front and centre' of our current thinking with regards to how we return to the days of the past. The 'review', and subsequent development of *Scotland United: A 2020 Vision,* summons us to move towards a new age of aspiration and ambition, an age of unashamed 'pursuit of excellence', where we rethink the way that we not only identify and manage talent but shift to a new mindset in how we 'value' it. In fact, so valuable is it that we're asked to afford it a 'prized and privileged' position in Scotland and treat it accordingly.

This new value system and mindset in relation to the importance and celebration of talent is said to be something relatively new in Scottish society. So important and implored are you to take the message seriously that the heading on page 28 of the 'review' reads: 'Talent, Talent, Talent' and has the following call to action:

> Above all else, this review urges a radical rethink of how we identify, manage, value and develop talent with emphasis on the 'gold dust' quality of elite young athletes and the intensity of attention and provision we must give them if their potential is to be realised for the benefit of Scottish Football, both the national and professional game. This is the distinguishing feature of comparisons between Scotland and our

more successful competitor countries. Despite our deep-seated cultural ambivalence in Scotland to success, elites and the talented – the 'we are a' Jock Thamson's bairns' concept – we must now break out of this and accept our success now depends on a new mindset and the unashamed pursuit of excellence: building the base, identifying the talent, and developing the potential.

There can be no doubt that, in modern society, to have 'talent' or be considered to be 'talented' is a desired quality. It's associated with money and fame. It's embedded in modern culture and has been popularised by shows such as *Britain's Got Talent* and the *X-Factor*-type 'talent' shows, those where you attempt to be discovered by showing off your talents. More significantly, in the life of young people and on social media platforms, talent has come to be associated with a world of supercars, lavish lifestyles and a sense of making it in the world. Talent, then, seems to hint at the chance of a better future, a type of life only afforded to the talented and all that comes with it.

If Scottish football is to experience this 'better life', the review urges that there's no time for an indifferent attitude towards those with a talent. In Scotland the term we're 'a' Jock Thamson's bairns' gets delivered to you, normally by someone your elder, as a reminder to you to not to get too big for your boots, or to stand out or show off. The review highlights that this cultural attitude is holding us back and is part of the 'tall poppy syndrome' that we need to break free from.

Tall poppy syndrome takes its name from the idea that gardeners trim down the tallest flowers to maintain a uniform look to their arrangements. More significantly, the metaphor has come to describe a societal attitude whereby a person's success and achievements are resented and criticised rather than celebrated, where society would rather disparage or cut them down to size for standing out. Its entry into the Scottish psyche seems to have a more Calvinistic lurking to it.[4] Perhaps to be a tall poppy, to stand out was associated with an unrighteousness and being at odds with a truer purpose of service to God. In Scottish society, the notion was that it might be better to 'hide your light under a bushel', to keep your abilities or qualities hidden for fear of being socially stigmatised or, even worse, ridiculed.

Instead of cutting them down to size, the review encourages that the 'gold dust' quality of the talented should hold a special regard in the 'intensity of attention and provision we must give them'. A move then towards a mindset of the unashamed pursuit of excellence. All part of the reward you should receive if you're 'identified' as being talented. Perhaps one of McLeish's clearest statements of this boldness was in his involvement in the creation of the (now disbanded) Fife Elite Football Academy, a collaboration of the professional clubs in Fife. I've no idea who came up with the name, but it makes a clear statement. This is an elite academy, and by implication these are the elite players, and we're not ashamed to say it! To embolden the sentiment further, on his appointment as chairman of the Fife collaboration and laced in the mindset of aspiration, ambition, achievement and performance, he would declare: 'I don't say this lightly, I want the Fife Elite Football Academy to be simply the best in Europe.'[5]

While the 'review' succeeded in leaving us in no doubt about the importance of talent and how we should view and treat it, despite over 170 references to 'talent' and/or 'talented', there appears to be no clear definition of the concept. The report does highlight the need for a clear definition of what 'terms' mean within youth development. Given the declaration of being unapologetic about the frequency of reference to the theme of talent, such a definition would have been a useful starting point. This isn't fleeting criticism or picking holes for the sake of it – System 1 is designed in the image of the talented child. We're encouraged to be unashamed about the celebration of it. It's a guiding concept, and the notion of it cascades through all aspects of today's youth footballing system – we should at least know what it is and what it isn't.

The concept of 'talent' is shaky, and the confusing messaging in the 'review' did little to alleviate this. For example, on one occasion we're reassured that 'talent does exist and there is no evidence to suggest this is not the case', and that 'exceptional talent should have a prized and privileged position in Scotland', and yet we are warned 'only a minority of youngsters who show initial signs of talent go on to become elite adult athletes'. This last acknowledgement is, of course, correct. Initial signs of talent are a poor predictor of future success and, as such, this is a reason why so few go on to fulfil their early 'potential' or talent. Given that so few who show an 'initial sign of talent' go on to succeed, it might not be all that wise to place so much emphasis on it.

In this sense, the 'review' seemed to simultaneously call for clearer definitions while using the theme of talent as the key focus for much of the change we need to see in the game. For the best part of the 19th and 20th centuries the main debate regarding talent has centred on what's known as the 'nature versus nurture' debate. It has given rise to sayings in favour of nature (natural ability), such as 'you've either got it or you haven't'; it's 'God given', a 'different breed', 'born to play', 'gifted', and many more expressions to suggest that it's possible to be born with a talent for a particular activity.

Nurture, on the other hand, suggests a more developmental approach to reaching a high level of performance. As we know, many apparently highly talented or gifted youngsters don't go on to reach elite adult levels of performance. This was the subject of interest of Benjamin Bloom, the influential professor of education, who led the project that investigated the developmental experiences of 121 of the best performers in fields such as sport, the arts, and music. Bloom concluded that irrespective of whether someone is talented or not, they need an intensive processes of encouragement, nurturance, education and training to reach the top.[6] However, this wasn't his major conclusion. After 40 years of intensive research in education settings, Bloom felt that the basic differences between humans are so small that 'what anyone in the world can learn, almost all persons can learn if provided with appropriate prior and current conditions of learning'. This further draws into question the focus and emphasis that has been put on the importance of 'talent'.

On one level, it matters little whether it's nature or nurture that's more important. It's a topic that's extensively researched, one that has dominated much of my professional life in conversations with parents, coaches and players, and has been the subject of many presentations I've given on the matter. The role and importance of talent is a divisive concept, let alone one that you would want as your guiding concept around which to build a national framework. What everyone agrees on is that without a long, intensive period of development, no individual will reach a high level of performance. As the 'review' highlights, if the pathways and models aren't in place, aligned to adequate facilities and opportunities, our potential will remain untapped. What we disagree on perhaps is 'who' gets selected, why they're getting selected and, as we'll come to see, the issue in relation to 'how many' get the 'golden ticket' of opportunity to participate in System 1.

As we can see, talent is an ambiguous and slippery term. Far too slippery to build solid foundations on. For example, a scout who unearths a 'talent' with a gift with the ball at their feet can know nothing about the talents of those around the individual, who for all we know may have a 'talent' for learning quickly or a 'talent' for working hard, both qualities that were found to be key characteristics of future high performers in Bloom's study. Someone may have a 'talent' for being calm under pressure (perhaps a single player may have a talent for learning, working hard and performing under pressure) or many other highly desirable qualities. However, at nine years old or even younger the concept of talent is typically associated with the demonstration of special physical qualities. It directs attention to those who 'stand out' – in this sense, as we'll come to see in Chapter 5, it's easy to spot the most talented ten-year-olds because what you're watching is essentially a physical illusion that's based on several contributing factors and, as such, we overlook other potentially more important attributes.

For now, and on a more concerning level, identifying and treating children as talented or gifted is also associated with negative psychological outcomes. 'Talented' individuals list in their top five of negatives the additional pressure that comes from teachers and parents. For players it can bring on anxiety created by raised expectations and, as told to me by one former pro-youth player, 'When I was selected for [...], everyone gets excited, your mum and dad, they tell everyone they know, you've been scouted so you must have talent, then you realise, you could also get released down the line – and that gets scary.' For the parents themselves, the worries can begin with identification anxiety, brought on by the realisation that there's only really a small window within which to realistically enter the system; once in the 'system', the worries shift to concerns about staying in and what lies ahead.

For players, however, getting recruited can just be the start of their worries. The initial excitement of being selected, the pressure of being monitored or not getting on with the coach, the obvious concerns about getting dropped from the programme, not getting that professional contract and day-to-day anxiety can turn into longer-term issues. Another former academy player told me about the paranoia that arises when a new player comes and you realise that they play in your position. You 'start to compare yourself to them, are they bigger, are they faster, can they do things I can't? You're continually looking over your shoulder.' Another told me about the issue with his size: 'I'd been the top player, but I wasn't growing, everyone was getting bigger than me, it got to the point I just couldn't keep up, and it became an issue for me.' It's part of life in System 1, where players are under no illusion that to stay in 'you need to work harder as you get older as there are fewer opportunities whereas there are a lot of younger children recruited'.[7]

These experiences are consistent with those identified by psychologist Carol Dweck, the American professor who coined the phrase 'growth mindset' to represent the best possible approach a learner can have to their development.[8] A fixed mindset is associated with the belief that talents are innate and, as such, fixed, while a growth mindset is associated with the belief that achievement is incrementally accrued through a process involving effort and feedback – a more positive attitude to development, if you like. Dweck found that those labelled as being talented were more likely to have a fixed mindset, believing that they had 'natural' talent. If talent is natural, then the enemy of this is 'effort'. This can create a sense., then, that if I must try hard, it somehow undermines the notion that I have 'natural' ability – effort is for the less talented.

At its worst, a fixed mindset has led to instances of cheating by individuals scared of losing their talented status to the extent of being reluctant to try new and more difficult challenges for fear of failure or being 'found out'. Either way, there's a demonstrable tendency to defend the initial judgement of being talented and guard against situations and outcomes that call this into question. It's perhaps not so important that as a nation we change our mindset towards talent; it may be that we need to consider more closely what the term does to the mindset of the individual labelled with it!

The 10,000 rule – not another shaky concept?

Moving on from the theme of talent and the unapologetic level of importance that the 'review' attributed to it. The 'review' also raises concerns about the skill level of Scottish players and then goes on to suggest how we go about rectifying this:

> The skill level of Scottish players is well below that of other comparable countries and Leagues. Young Scots spend less time practicing [sic] with a ball than those in Portugal, France, Holland and Spain and the average hours per week developing technical skills, is much lower in Scotland.

The solution, according to the 'review', is that:

> We need to establish the 10,000 hours standard for top class skill development … The 10,000 hours issue remains an international benchmark for top-class skill development. There is need for deliberate practice and play over a 10 year period (3 hours a day). This is associated with expert international levels of performance.

The 10,000 hours standard, as it's put, is more commonly known as the 10,000-hour 'rule' (10k rule). To date, in the 21st century, no other idea, theme or concept has made a bigger impact on talent development than this one. Quite simply, the 10k rule argues that those who practise longer and to a greater level of intensity eventually become the best in their field. Like Bloom, the 10k rule proposed that to get really good at something, so good as to be called an 'expert', is less about talent but instead is the end result of 'deliberate practice' extended for a minimum of ten years.

So simple was the message that it became instantly appealing to the mass media and was popularised by books such as Geoff Colvin's *Talent is Overrated* (2008), Malcolm Gladwell's *Outliers* (2009) and Daniel Coyle's *The Talent Code* (2009). Where then did these authors get the concept from and what have the implications been for the world of sport and, indeed, talent development? The concept dates to 1993 and a Swedish professor of psychology by the name of Anders Ericsson. Along with his colleagues, Ericsson compared the practice habits of expert musicians attending the Music Academy of West Berlin to those of non-expert musicians and concluded that a key factor differentiating the groups lay in the greater number of hours the experts spent practising compared to the non-experts. The hours accumulated by the expert musicians showed that it took three hours per day of 'deliberate practice' for ten years – and this gave rise to the 10k rule.

By Ericsson's own admission in 2020, one of the biggest problems with applying the concept to sport is that the structure of training instrumental musicians is very different to that typically available to athletes.[9] Not surprisingly, studies have shown that elite athletes rarely accumulate this number of hours before reaching international levels of performance. Available research in football has consistently shown the number of hours needed to become elite to be significantly lower than 10,000. One of the most striking features of the 10k rule is that we now know that some reach elite level of performance well before ten years or 10,000k hours. In fact, some even accumulate more years and more hours and still never become elite. In Germany, research has shown that elite players made their debut in the Bundesliga after 4,264 hours of deliberate practice, and national team debuts were reached by 4,532 hours.[10] Meanwhile, research from the Norwegian School of Sport Sciences found that while the professional players in their study accumulated more hours at all ages between 6 and 19 than the non-professional players, there wasn't a significant difference between the groups.[11]

One of the key problems of aligning to a theory of ten years is that it drives the notion that the earlier a child starts the better, particularly when the UEFA Club Licensing System requires clubs to have teams from U10 upwards. The quicker you begin deliberate practice the more likely it is that you'll gain an advantage over someone the same age who starts later. If you have two ten-year-olds and child 'A' starts focused and consistent practice at five years old, and child 'B' starts at ten, who do you think is going to selected by a talent scout if they're both on the same pitch during an U11 match? Starting early improves your chances of being scouted into System 1. Parents have come to value the 'early start' because it essentially gives their child a 'head start', and this is what's known in TID as 'early specialisation'.

This reinforces the earlier point that if you're going to be good enough to get into a performance school at the age of 11, you'll probably have to have been good enough to be with a professional club since the age of nine. This essentially means your footballing development will have started many years before. If the 'talent' theory aligned to the 10k rule worked, then a nine-year-old child entering System 1 would be ready for the first team at 19 – and yet this is seldom the case!

Hurry up, the bus is leaving soon – early specialisation versus early diversification

When it comes to early specialisation, it's not difficult to find examples to seemingly validate the approach. Four years after the research that gave rise to the 10k rule, Tiger Woods became the youngest winner of the US Masters (one of golf's four major championships), and later that year he went on to become the number-one golfer in the world. Woods dominated the first decade of the 21st century in professional golf, winning 12 of his 14 majors.

Footage soon emerged of Woods displaying his golfing talents on TV when he was only two years old. A new narrative was developing in youth development. In *Talent is Overrated*, Geoff Colvin proposes that Tiger wasn't born a genius, instead his success was in part due to the fact that he started 'deliberate' practice from a very young age. Around the same time, the Williams sisters, Serena and Venus, were becoming the dominant players in tennis. They had both turned professional at 14 and had both won a grand slam by 17 – it's well publicised that they started playing at just three. Not only this, both Tiger and the Williams sisters had fathers who were extremely proactive in driving their development.

We now had a good fit between Ericsson's theory and high-profile examples of the effect in action, especially as the theory had suggested that because it took at least ten years to become good, the best approach was to start as early as possible and to focus exclusively on one activity. Furthermore, practice is said to be 'deliberate practice' when it's intensive, specialised, coach-led and is being monitored. Again, we appeared to have a good fit between the 'theory' and what was believed to be true about the development histories of Woods and the Williams sisters. In fact, so good was the fit that the 10k rule would dominate thinking in TID well into the second decade of the new century.

Elite systems around the world, across many different sports that are aligned to this approach, have essentially created a 'model' that has left young players 'competing' for limited spaces in elite programmes. It has elements of 'survival of the fittest' to it – Charles Darwin's theory of evolution – the sooner you start training and practising the more developed your skills will be when compared to your later-starting peers and the more likely you'll be to get to the front of the queue.

This 'competitive model' is analogous to a child trying to get on a busy bus. To get on the elite bus, you need to be quick. It tends to leave early, so a parent will probably drive you to the bus stop. If you miss the bus, you'll be left back in System 2 and there's no telling when the next bus will be. Not only that, when the next bus comes there might be more people waiting for it and they might be bigger, stronger, faster and push their way to the front ahead of you; even worse – they might change the route and it doesn't come by your way again, so you're left here for good. What are you going to do then? For some it's simple: a parent will drop them off at the new bus route and they can try to get on it there! For others, their talents might well be lost to the system for evermore.

Early specialisation works for some, the celebrated exponents of it are testament to that. However, we hear nothing about those who followed the 10k rule, started early and practised for many, many years and yet didn't make it. For these youngsters there are factors at play that further complicate the issue. We also hear almost nothing about other potentially more effective approaches.

It may be asked: why should we pay attention to these approaches? Especially as System 1 seems to be set up in the image of the 'competitive model' – and this concept follows the early specialisation approach. Well, some of the greatest sportspeople of all time have followed a counter-approach called 'early diversification'. In this approach the future elite performer has specialised in their sport later, instead taking part in a diverse range of different activities. Prior to late specialisation they engaged in a period of what has become known as 'deliberate play'. Significantly, this is activity that's deliberately not coach-led, instead the activity is regulated by the participants and is undertaken for the enjoyment of the activity rather than for the purposes of improving performance. Notably, the approach has been shown to foster the intrinsic motivation to engage for long periods in an activity, which in turn can create the physical conditioning and other key skills associated with elite-level performance. All-time greats associated with such an approach are the likes of Roger Federer, Michael Jordan, Wayne Gretzky, Michael Phelps and Scotland's Sir Chris Hoy.[12]

If the current 'competitive model' of System 1 has created a rush to specialise early, then how does this compare to the 20th century and early part of the 21st? Before 'the achterbankgeneratie', it was a time of more natural growth, and specialisation would occur later, when 'talents' had been confirmed. Early years in Scottish life were less characterised by parental involvement. If you missed the bus you had to walk home, probably kicking a ball or a can or anything that could be kicked! Early specialisation to the exclusion of other activities wasn't common. It was a time where 'play' was more the order of the day to fill the long hours of non-school-based activity. Activities such as street football, hide and seek, tig, perhaps, for some involvement in various sports. Andy Murray was offered a trial with Rangers at 15, before making the decision to specialise in tennis, while Andy Robertson was the junior captain at Cathcart Castle Golf Club and had a 5 handicap at the age of 15.

For those that did specialise in football at an early age, it's likely that they were engaged in what's known as 'diversification within specialisation'. This simply means that while football dominated their lives from an early age, their experiences of the game would be highly diverse. Not only that, but large amounts of the activity would be informal in nature and not organised by an adult. This could involve playing on the streets, various grass areas, playing with older boys as well as younger ones; playing with your local boys' team as well as your school team; or if there was no one else about, playing keepie-uppie or any other activity for the pure intrinsic joy of playing. This simply means that your experience of a single sport was diverse and less structured.

Barry Ferguson recalls a childhood of obsessive involvement in football from a young age.[13] His early footballing experiences were varied and diverse and driven out of an internal love of playing the game. At the age of seven he was already playing against older boys at Lawmuir Primary School. He recalls neighbouring 'schemes' playing matches on pitches marked out with sawdust, goalposts made from scrap wood, on a pitch they had mown themselves, and of evenings spent kicking a ball about under streetlights. All this is in stark contrast to the growing concerns of the regimented, adult-organised programmes, perpetual training cycles that are characterised by early specialisation, and increased parental involvement. Not surprisingly, Ferguson argues that 'today's youths have gone soft, but I don't blame them. I blame the system they are being brought up in.'

Specialised or diversified? What does the science say?

The subject of early versus late specialisation is one of great academic interest. Alongside nature versus nurture, it's among the most debated topics in youth sport. Professor Arne Güllich is a sports scientist and researcher at Technical University of Kaiserslautern, in Germany. He has published over 100 peer-reviewed articles. Güllich and his colleagues published a study in 2022 that set out to explain the acquisition of exceptional human performance and particularly to set out what's known in relation to the different approaches. They looked at data from 51 studies that included 6,096 athletes, of which 772 were world-class. They were specifically interested in: 1) the age the athlete started their main sport; 2) the age they reached significant milestones; 3) how much coach-led practice they had and how much youth-led play (informal games) they had in their main sport and other sports. What they found, not surprisingly when it comes to age-group performance, was that those who started earlier and practised more were the top performers. However, when it came to the athletes that had gone on to be world-class, they started their main sport later and instead had engaged in more childhood/adolescent multisport practice, causing them to initially progress more slowly.

The findings above demonstrate that multisport practice from an early age was a greater predictor of future performance level than starting early and only focusing on one sport. Those who started to specialise in the sport and later became famous for doing so started at a later age than those who didn't reach their performance level. On the occasion that an early specialiser did start early and reach a world-class level, this was shown to be the exception rather than the rule. The counter argument here is easy to predict. Those who go on 'today' to reach a high level of football in Scotland do so by specialising early, and they do so by showing the 'talent' associated with early selection into the pro-youth academy system. I doubt very much that there's an argument against this.

That, however, isn't the take-home here. If we know that the characteristics and attributes needed to be world-class are acquired via a different pathway, then we have a problem. Firstly, the elite system doesn't currently for the most part produce world-class players. If most players in System 1 are early specialisers and go on to become professional players, this in itself doesn't validate the approach. If the elite system isn't producing top-class performers, capable of playing for any team, in any league, then the opposite in fact must be closer to the truth. Secondly, the only viable entry to professional football in Scotland is via System 1, which essentially makes it very difficult for anyone taking an alternative approach to enter professional football, never mind become world-class or show their *talent, talent, talent*!

Chapter 5

Review of 'the review' – Part 2: The rich get richer, the poor get poorer

TO IMPLEMENT the recommendations of the 'review', 103 in total across Part 1 and Part 2, the SFA published its new performance strategy, entitled *Scotland United: A 2020 Vision*.[1] The opening statement of the vision declares: 'January 12, 2011. It is a date that should be remembered as the day the Scottish FA took its first steps towards the most radical overhaul in its 138-year history.'

With the case now made that the international standard for skill development was the 10k rule, it was time to set about putting in place a system that could deliver on this benchmark. To provide a platform for the delivery of such quantity of practice, a key recommendation was that: 'The Scottish FA should establish Schools of Football/Football Academies based on developing centres of excellence – at least 20 comprehensive school-based models which are integrated into the school curriculum.'

The report had highlighted that in every major European football set-up, education and football is intertwined. Barcelona were identified as having the 'best youth system in the world'. Their approach of combining football and education was highlighted, as this afforded the players the opportunity to spend more time with the ball at their feet. Messi was quoted as saying, 'At Barça we trained every day with the ball, I hardly ever ran without a ball at my feet. It was a form of training aimed very clearly at developing your skills.'

Around the same time as the report was being developed, Barcelona were dominating world football. In 2008/9 they won the Champions League, La Liga and the Copa del Rey. The team of 2010 were perhaps the greatest club team ever, featuring nine players who had come through the club's youth system. This included the likes of Puyol, Messi, Xavi, Busquets, Iniesta – not just products of the youth systems but icons of the game. Not surprisingly, La Masia, the club's academy, had become the 'champions model' of the day. This is based on the assumption that the most successful team of the day had hit on a winning formula and, as such, it made sense for others to adopt a similar approach.

More than a decade on from the publication of the 'review', things haven't gone as well for the Catalonian giants. They've won the Champions League on only one more occasion, and been beyond the quarter-finals on one other occasion. In 2022/23 they didn't qualify for the Champions League and instead competed in the Europa League. They're no longer the 'champions model' and, on reflection, the team of 2009 to 2011 seems to have had more to do with the beliefs of the man who was to become the coach. In 2008, after a string of bad results, the Barcelona B team coach, Pep Guardiola, was put in charge of the first team. A product of the Barcelona 'system' himself, Pep was said to believe that the biggest victory was to give a La Masia player their debut. This says more about a commitment to youth than it does for the system of developing them.

With the justification now clear, and with what appears to be strong evidence from Europe's biggest clubs, the creation of a system to integrate education with football would become a key priority. With no time to waste, the radical overhaul saw point 13 from the 'review' implemented with the appointment of the Dutchman, Mark Wotte to the role of SFA Performance Director. The remit of the new post was clear:

> Oversee our ambitious new academy network and have a direct role in the development of youth talent and elite athletes. The aim of our new approach should be to deal with emerging talent and to raise the technical ability of players across all levels of the game through training and lifestyle development of boys and girls.

In 2012, the SFA launched their new performance schools programme. The performance schools were intended to link football academies to education, and heralded this new mindset in the pursuit of excellence. The schools currently operate in seven key regions: Hazlehead Academy in Aberdeen, St John's RC High School in Dundee, Broughton High School in Edinburgh, Graeme High School in Falkirk, Holyrood Secondary School in Glasgow, Grange

Academy in Kilmarnock, and Braidhurst High School in Motherwell. Today, each school has a full-time elite coach across their four years of schooling, school attendees receive an extra 800 hours of coaching and this is delivered during school hours. Each programme is further supported by national team coaches, sport scientists and other specialist experts.[2]

On his appointment, Wotte put his own stamp on the 2020 vision, targeting representation of performance school graduates in the national squad for the Euro 2020 finals. He told the media, 'When we're in 2020 and we have four or five top players with a performance school history, we'll have done a great job. That's the goal. In 2020 come and chat to me again about it.' When Steve Clarke named his 26-man squad for the 2020 Euros, Nathan Patterson, who was breaking through at Rangers ahead of his move to Everton, and Billy Gilmour, who was with Chelsea at the time, were both named in the squad – and notably they were also performance school graduates. The vision, for some, had been realised.

The extent to which performance schools have helped to elevate the 'gold dust' quality of Scotland's elite to new levels is hard to tell. The slightly older Kieran Tierney and David Turnbull also made the squad; both are highly rated. Had they been a couple of years younger they would probably have entered the SFA's performance school system. Would this have made them better players? The same goes for the other 23 members of that squad. Had they been younger and geographically able, would they have been better players for having a performance school experience? They all had to go to school somewhere, in the same way as

Jimmy Johnstone, Kenny Dalglish, Jim Baxter and all the other greats did. The question is this: are the performance schools producing players of the quantity and quality that will return us to the golden age and 'elevate us' as a football nation? Not just contribute players into the first teams of our professional clubs and occasionally our national team.

When trying to establish the efficacy of any talent development system – be it La Masia or the performances schools – it's difficult to say what works, what doesn't or what really makes a difference. When we celebrate the progression of performance school graduates into senior professional football, we celebrate for the wrong reason. In these instances it suggests a 'desire to have been right' that's associated with several cognitive biases, including *confirmation bias*, and *survivorship bias*. This isn't just an issue in Scottish football, as cognitive biases tend to exist wherever we've made selections and our methods are under scrutiny. It can be seen across all levels of the talent development system, in all sports across the world.

When it comes to *confirmation bias*, this is our tendency to cherry-pick information and present it as evidence to validate our approach. In the case of Kieran Tierney, you might argue that his involvement with the Celtic/ St Ninian's High School collaboration was a factor in his success; however, you might fail to mention that he moved there from Our Lady's High School in Motherwell – a school that the likes of Billy McNeil, Bobby Murdoch and Sir Matt Busby went to. Which one was more responsible for his development? We might highlight Billy Gilmour and Nathan Patterson as performance school successes but choose to ignore all the classmates who haven't risen to their level; this is the classic cognitive shortcut known as *survivorship bias*, where we only concentrate on those who make it and dismiss those who don't. When it comes to celebrating the success of those who appear to be products of a system, it works along similar lines as this: 'Select some eggs. Put eggs in a plastic bag. Throw the plastic bag at a wall. Show the world the egg that doesn't break – the system works.' (Anon).

Those who survive are then used as the benchmark for those coming behind – the system works! The problem is, how do you prove that this is true? What constitutes a system that works? The 'historical' system of the 20th century produced a volume of high-quality players to suggest that the 'system' – whatever that was – worked! For something to be considered as 'working' it needs to produce a consistent result. If that consistent result isn't the one you were expecting then it's reasonable to suggest that there's something not right. As such we need to break out of the default position that many elite youth programmes take, that when a player 'makes it' the suggestion is that the system 'produced' that player – they become a 'celebrated' product of that 'system'. When they don't make it, the reason given is more likely to be the player didn't do what the academy asked of them! They didn't follow instruction! They didn't work hard enough! They had a bad attitude! Which all suggests that they 'just don't have what its takes'. In other words, if they had just copied what the 'star' player had done at their age, all would have worked out fine.

Typically, any system set up on this basis will look to blame the individual rather than the system when a 'talented' player doesn't go on to 'make it'. The exact same issue exists with the 10k 'deliberate practice' methodology. When a performer follows the system and it works, they validate the system, but when the opposite happens, it's easy to say they didn't follow the key aspects of the method, so don't blame the method. The problem as I see it is that the system is set up in such a way that it creates this problem. In doing so it places unrealistic expectations on those working in the system, such as coaches and heads of performance. They're working with the system that has been given to them and there are many factors that are interacting to work against them.

The truth is that players such as Kieran Tierney, Callum MacGregor, Billy Gilmour and perhaps the type of talent that Nathan Patterson will turn out to be are 'outliers' in every sense imaginable. An outlier means they're abnormally different from others in the same population they've come from. This means they don't represent the statistical norm of what the system typically produces and therefore can't be used to represent the system. They are, in fact, so far from the 'norm' that there's nothing that those in the 'system' can learn from their development that will be any use to them.

As we'll come to see, there's much that can be learned from the likes of Andy Robertson, although he may also be seen as an outlier. However, he's far more representative of the 'norm' than those mentioned above. Robertson was making his way in System 1, then he was released by Celtic and played down the divisions with Queen's Park. Hundreds have followed a similar path in their careers. No one could have predicted the trajectory he would take from there. It would be interesting to know what cognitive biases have been used to explain his release from Celtic. Robertson did something remarkable that many before him and after him couldn't but it could just have easily worked out differently for him. At 18 he famously tweeted, 'Life at this age is rubbish with no money #needajob.'

For now, the biggest issue isn't what System 1 is or isn't doing for those players in it. The implications for those not in the system is a bigger factor, which quite literally gets bigger by the day. There's a strange but explainable phenomenon (both physically and mentally) that takes place when we you remove the most 'talented' from the 'big' talent pool (System 2) and create a separate, smaller elite pool (System 1). This modern methodology connects our current problems to the 'non' system of the past. It's one of the reasons why I think the conditions of the last century were so successful – and we could fix this overnight! Let's look at this more closely ...

The rich get richer, the poor get poorer !

According to McLeish, his case for the future of Scottish football largely rested on the view of young people as 'football capital' as they represent the 'wealth' of the game.[3] The association of 'talent' with capital and wealth dates back to the Greek word *tálanton*, which means 'balance, weight, sum of money'. In Ancient Greece, talent was originally a unit of weight (equivalent to 25.86 kilograms) then ultimately became a 'coin'. One talent was worth 60 minas or 6,000 drachmas, a substantial amount of money when you consider the average wage at the time was 3.5 drachmas. Not surprisingly then, 'talents' were something that only rich people had.[4] Perhaps this is where the notion that when it comes to talent, you've either 'got it or you haven't' comes from.

As far back as the 'Parable of the Talents' in Matthew 25:14–30, from the New Testament, the story is told of a master who entrusts his property to his three servants.[5] According to their abilities, one received five talents, the second two and the third only one. After a lengthy absence, the master returns to find the first and second men have put their talents to work and doubled their value – they're duly rewarded. The third man, however, had hidden his talent by burying it in the ground – he instead was punished. As it goes:

> Take therefore the talent from him, and give it unto him which hath ten talents. For unto every one that hath shall be given, and he shall have abundance: but from him, that hath not shall be taken away even that which he hath. And cast ye the unprofitable servant into outer darkness: there shall be weeping and gnashing of teeth. (Matthew 25:24–30)

Hidden talent was worthless then and it's worthless today. Those who are perceived to have greater ability and put that ability to use are rewarded by receiving more. Those of less perceived ability are given less and are punished for not showing what they can do with their more limited starting point. In reality, this can begin in the home with a parent's initial perception of their child's ability. A parent may only need to think they have a talented child for that child to receive extra resources and attention, which accumulate over time and create bigger advantages, so big that it becomes difficult for the slower starter to catch up.

In football, at the point of selection into an elite academy programme and/or a performance school, a point of separation begins in the journey of the young player and the journey of those not selected. That separation now sets the youngster on a System 1 or System 2 pathway in the game. If you're in System 1 you're on the path of abundance; however, if you find yourself in System 2, it can be more like being cast into outer darkness – especially if your aspirations are to be a professional player. This is what American sociologist Robert Merton termed the 'Matthew Effect', and he coined the phrase based on the previously mentioned verse from the parable. More precisely, it was the name he gave to his 'cumulative advantage/disadvantage theory' to describe the commonly observed tendency for an initial advantage to accumulate through time to a time when 'success breeds success' and where 'the rich get richer, and the poor get poorer'.[6]

Youngsters selected into System 1 will quickly find themselves on the correct side of the Matthew Effect. Here the advantage of being selected interacts with training and opportunity to produce a larger development effect than those players who didn't show the same initial potential. As we've already highlighted, that early advantage may have been accrued because of one individual beginning specialisation earlier and, as such, they're already at a more advanced stage. Or as we'll come to see, the initial advantage could be biological in nature – or even be down to what month of the year you're born in. Nevertheless, soon the accumulation of these advantages means that it's not that difficult to stay ahead of their System 2 friends, hence turnover of academy players appears to be relatively small. The Matthew Effect is in full flow, early advantage begets future advantage, and it does so in a disproportionate manner – the rich are getting richer, while the poor get poorer.

The system is set up in such a way that it's highly likely that anyone reaching a high level of professional football will follow the Matthew pattern. That pattern is one in which the small initial advantage is going to multiply over a decade of intense specialised experiences. This could involve the accumulation of the advantage of both involvement with a professional club and being an attendee at a performance school. As highlighted in one of the early updates from the SFA:

> The creation of our seven Regional Performance Schools has also been a major breakthrough. Over the four years of the project, the Scottish FA will have identified and cultivated almost 500 of the country's most promising talents, both girls and boys, from 12 years old and with the help of their clubs provide an additional eight hours of quality skills development for each young player: an essential boost in the quest to achieve the established 10,000 hours of practice to achieve excellence.

Yes, an essential boost! But only for those whose development has been amplified by the chain reaction of advantages afforded to those in System 1. The Matthew

Effect creates a 'virtuous' circle for those selected, but for those not selected it becomes more a 'vicious' circle. In the 'virtuous circle' you're strongly rewarded for your perceived abilities.[7] No such boost, however, for those left behind in System 2. They may aspire to join System 1, but they're now part of a 'vicious circle' of underachievement afforded to them for not demonstrating the 'initial' talent to enter System 1 – from here on in their chances of joining the premium system are slim! A vicious circle follows the same pattern as the virtuous circle, but they have divergent paths. One accumulates wealth and the other poverty. Whatever their initial ability, the odds of proper development for those in the vicious circle sink drastically and the odds of further failure increase by the same amount.

In System 1, not only do they receive more coaching, but it also follows that they receive better coaching. Here the coaches are more experienced and are qualified to a higher level. To work in the elite system, you'll typically need a UEFA Elite A youth licence or a UEFA A licence. To reach these levels of qualification involves working through all the various lower levels of coaching before undertaking a rigorous and intensive process of tasks, assignments, visits and reports – not surprisingly for those who reach this level, coaching is most likely their main job. This is unlike System 2, where it's largely run by volunteers who do significant and valuable work. For the most part the coaches will undertake basic qualifications to meet the criteria set by the SFA. Within the hierarchy of the two systems the best coaches work with the 'perceived' best children in System 1; the least qualified work with everyone else. The 'talent monopolises the resources – the gap widens!

It's true to say that everyone in System 1 and System 2 has a chance to succeed, but it's a statistical fallacy to say everyone has an equal chance. The author Daniel Rigney highlights this fallacy by comparing the situation to a game of Monopoly. According to Rigney, if two identical twins with the same talent and effort play Monopoly but one starts with more resources, that twin almost always wins.[8] It means that we're currently in a situation in Scotland where we 'can' say that everyone has an opportunity to succeed, but we 'can't' say that everyone has an equal opportunity to succeed. In Scotland, in 2023, youngsters are playing a skewed game of Monopoly in their endeavours to become professional footballers – and all because of the shaky currency of talent!

Sharks on the streets

When it comes to linking the development conditions of the past to the present, the role of the street and street football is never far from the discussion. It keeps reoccurring and will continue to do so. We've already talked about the conditions of the street in making the 'real' game easier, and how this relates to the development of the positive psychological flow-like state. The role of street football also wasn't lost on McLeish in the 'review' or his notion that somehow it contained crucial conditions that needed to be retained to produce better players:

> We cannot recreate street football in the old meaning of the phrase but we can create the conditions in which that level of familiarity with the ball alongside the development of natural

ability and skills can take place – providing the benefits deriving from the old game but in a modern context.

I don't know what McLeish believed those conditions to be or how they would be recreated. I'm not sure if that line of thought was followed through; perhaps the information exists or at least is part of the information those working in System 1 have access to – perhaps not! However, it's an important line of thought to develop and follow through on. I think it's critical to our understanding of what we had, and what we've lost – and food for thought on what we do about it!

Make no mistake, the Matthew Effect also existed on the streets, as it does in all areas of life (obesity is highest in the richest countries). In a stimulus-rich environment such as the 'street', those with an early advantage were able to exploit the conditions. Whatever that early advantage was, be it they were bigger, stronger, more aggressive, more confident or had been playing longer, the advantage existed in one form or another. It can't not! Those with an advantage would get more of the ball. It could be for any number of reasons. Perhaps they could win it more easily, team-mates passed to them more often, opposition players stood off them. Not only that, but they also get more praise and positive reinforcement about their ability. They play more matches, as they're more readily accepted in older age groups – again more positive reinforcement – and from there they most likely join the best boys' teams.

However, for the best part of the previous century they weren't removed from the 'talent' pool as early, then hot-housed with those 'like' them and separated from everyone else. By keeping them in the talent pool longer it created a 'path' of diversity rather than one of 'separation', and this most benefited the weaker players. Let's just say that you merge System 1 and 2 together into one big system; there would still be a Matthew Effect. The early stronger players would still dominate for a time, and they would likely get more game time and be the favourites of the coaches. That's not the point. The point is what it does for all those around them. The effect on the weaker children is likely to be the same as in the playground or on the streets. They must develop new skills to survive or work harder – because they have to – and this is the path of diversity. This is what I call the powerful influence of a creating a 'because I had to' culture.

In a path of separation for System 1 players there's a lack of diversity for the best players. But here's where it gets interesting. It follows that there must also be a Matthew Effect within the elite system, and the pattern above repeats itself. The players in the academy system, the 'really' highly rated ones, even though the system may be set up for their benefit, often don't fulfil their potential, and the same reason applies. Instead, it's a 'shirt filler' that surprises everyone and makes the breakthrough. These, 'shirt fillers' are still good players, and there on merit, but they're not the top prospects.

I was introduced to the term 'shirt fillers' by an academy coach who had come into our club to run sessions for our System 2 team. Not the greatest phrase in the world but this is what he used. It describes how you construct a team around your top talents. He explained you might have two boys in an age group who you genuinely think might make it, but you need eleven players to play a match, so the other nine (plus subs) are 'shirt fillers' for the benefit of the few. Again, the Matthew pattern can be seen here. However, it doesn't serve the top prospect all that well, and the problem is we don't know about it until it's too late.

All the while, the lesser players are experiencing better development conditions because they're forced to develop new qualities and skills. These new skills or attributes may come in the form of trickery, guile, deception, cunning, quicker reaction time – the list could go on and on. How many times have you heard it said in a conversation about a player who 'makes it' from a certain area or club that 'they weren't even the best player', that 'such and such' was a far better player when they were younger; 'what a player he could have been!' That's because the player who 'made it' needed the conditions that the stronger one created to aid their development.

The better players at an age-group level aren't experiencing the same tension and stress and now the accumulation of early advantage has been reversed and becomes a disadvantage. When you have tension and stress you get adaptation. As James 'Doc' Counsilman, the Olympic Hall of Fame swimming coach puts it: 'We are what we are because of stresses placed upon us and the adaptations we have made to these stresses both physical and otherwise. The state of our bodies, our minds, and our personalities is the result of these adaptations.'

Counsilman knew a thing or two about training people to become world-class performers. He was the head coach of the United States men's swimming team that won 9 out of 11 gold medals at the Tokyo Games in 1964 and 12 out of 13 at the 1976 Montreal Games. The two medals he didn't win were won by two Australian swimmers who he coached at Indiana University.[9] Stress can sound like an undesirable condition and an unusual one to introduce into a conversation about youth development. Replace the word 'stress' with the word 'challenge' and we have the same thing. When it's used appropriately it's our most powerful tool, and as humans it's our developmental super power.

Take, for example, endurance athletes. They very often experience enlarged hearts, which speeds up the flow of blood to meet their increased need for oxygen. Why? Because it has to! A professional keyboard player can produce 1,800 notes per minute with a level of precision that's unsurpassed in any other type of human behaviour; this is possible because through specific training they develop quicker nerve conduction.[10] Unless you've trained to be a musician or an endurance runner you won't share these physical characteristics – because you don't need them! In other words, the mechanisms of the body, through training, adapt to meet the demands that are being placed on them – the fancy term is 'gene expression' – and that's how appropriate stress and challenge works!

In their excellent book, *Youth Development in Football*, Mark Nesti and Chris Sulley tell the anecdote that they picked up from a member of the recruitment staff at Barcelona in relation to why they like to have foreign players in their older squads. This essentially describes how stress and challenge in the talent pool works:

The Japanese people have a real liking for tuna fish and this has led to stocks around the world to fall and the price to rise, therefore the Japanese decided to farm their own. However, what they found was that because they weren't in the wild and subject to the stress of predators the meat became less palatable. By trial and error, they discovered by introducing sharks into their habitat it stressed the tuna and the meat became high quality again but had to accept that they might have to lose 10% of their stock.[11]

This is a little like how the conditions of the street worked in the past. It wasn't that it was the initially stronger players who necessarily made it to the top; they were the 'sharks' that stressed out the other inhabitants. For some the stress was too much and they wouldn't return, a natural consequence of the wild, but there was an equal volume waiting in the wings to fill their space. The ones who did keep coming back for more were the ones that would go on to develop superior and sought-after skills. Why? Because they had to! Just imagine recreating this situation today, where the 'early' strong players are there because they're most needed to produce the desired skills and attributes in the initially weaker players. Of course, it has to be done in the correct way and done in a way that's beneficial to all. You can never really know what you'll get in these cultures – but you do know you won't get the same old thing!

Final thoughts

While we can't say the streets created professional footballers out of everyone who played on them – far more didn't become professionals than did – what we can say is that when it did, it created better players than the system produces today. An understanding of the Matthew Effect, its patterns and potential, should be part of any discussion on how we recreate 'the benefits deriving from the old game but in a modern context'. Before that can happen we need to work through several other inefficiencies that exist when you follow a path of separation on the journey to elite performance. For now, it's time we considered reintroducing the sharks to the 'talent' pool for the benefit of all in the eco-system of youth development!

Chapter 6

Talent identification and selection

THE PROCESS of talent identification is that of identifying and then selecting the most promising young players from the population in the hope that they can develop into future first-team players. Not only does this have the potential to enhance the playing squad, but they may even show a return on investment if they're sold on. Players who do neither join the statistics of those for which the system didn't do what it set out to do. It's not just an issue in football, it's an issue in any sport that makes early selections into elite programmes. For example, studies have shown that in athletics only 2 per cent of youth athletes come through the talent pathways to achieve international honours as a senior, while in rugby union 76 per cent of those who competed at a national level at U13 weren't competing nationally at U18.[1]

In football, at one elite-level professional academy in Scotland, researchers from Robert Gordon University tracked 512 players from the U10–U17 age groups across ten years. By the end of the study, 362 of them had been released and didn't attain professional status at their parent or any other club.[2] Similarly, researchers at the University of Stirling tracked youth soccer players affiliated to a top-tier Scottish academy from 2006 until 2017. Only 53 out of the 537 players in the study were successful in obtaining a senior professional contract by the time they graduated from the academy at U17 level.[3]

Not only does this indicate that on nine out of ten occasions the stated aim wasn't achieved, but an underlying and more significant issue plays out in the background. The reality is far further-reaching than just looking at the data on who was selected or didn't make it. This ignores a significant additional error – that for every youngster who was successfully selected into the elite academy system and didn't make it, at least one other youngster (but probably two, three or even more) will have been considered but not selected. This minimally doubles the selection error. As Professor Ross Tucker puts it, not only have you made an inclusion error, but you've made an exclusion error.[4]

The facts and figures above are alarming. Even more alarming is that they only tell us about the journey to senior football – the point where a player's career is just beginning. We haven't yet got to the likelihood of a player progressing through their parent academy and making a significant contribution to the first team – that's a whole other matter, but one we'll return to. So complex is it that if the efficacy of TI was based on successful outcomes and subject to the same rigour as the medical profession, the industry might be shut down.

This is no fault of those working in System 1 and tasked with the job. Their goal is well intended. It's to find the talent, place it in the system and then develop it into future elite-level performance. This is what the job asks of them!

As is often cited, the problem in life, as in football, is that 'you do not rise to the level of your goals, you fall to the level of your systems'.[5] The system asks you to select early, to pick the best performers and to place them in a best vs best environment. However, if the system is flawed, at some point things are going to go wrong.

Scouting for 'talent'

When it comes to scouting players into System 1, the process starts in the years leading up to the first major intake. This happens at around nine years old, the year before and in preparation for the official club academy programme to start. This is in itself a substantial task, as there are around 68,500 young people registered as players across more than 4,000 clubs. To get players of outstanding ability and talent into the elite system, most clubs operate a large scouting network, both formal and informal, that will cover matches and tournaments across the country. This will include coaches at key boys' clubs and the use of trusted sources in the various geographical talent hotbeds. The best possible scenario for a scout is when the same name keeps coming up from multiple sources.

The elite system appears to operate with around 2,500 players; however, only a small percentage of new players come into this system each year. Largely speaking, these are the boys who will fill the youngest age-group teams. So, while there might be 2,500 boys in System 1 at any given point, only a relatively small number of places need be filled on a yearly basis. For example, if the system only needs 300 new players every year, this represents as little as around 0.5 per cent of the overall talent pool available from those registered across our grassroots clubs. We need to decide whether this intense focus on so few is working for us or against us.

Numbers aside, from experience, regardless of what team the scout or contact represents, the process appears to work along these lines. Representatives will attend matches most Saturday or Sunday mornings, particularly at historically fertile selection grounds where the best local players have already been recruited into a successful year-on-year team so therefore half the job has already been done for the scout. Some parents will also try to put their children in the shop window by identifying the teams where kids get scouted from and actively pursue a spot in this team. They've realised early that talent is worth nothing if it's hidden away. However, and by whatever means a child gets on the radar of a scout, a final decision will only be made after an extended trial where they'll be compared to other 'identified' players.

According to Craig Mulholland, the former head of Rangers' academy, 'If you don't get that bit right, at U10s, you're always chasing it the whole way through, year after year.'[6] Mulholland explains that Rangers have a:

> player grading model, there's a pipeline of talent all the way from U11 all the way through to the B team, and then what we do is look at where the gaps occur and where do we need to recruit into those gaps to make sure we always have enough 'A' players in the system we can push forward towards the first team.

In this sense the system stays open and there are opportunities to come into it later.

When it comes to scouting into these gaps, naturally, clubs need to find players of an appropriate standard and, as such, a decision will involve a comparison to what's already in the elite system. For example, at Hearts, if you're invited in for a trial the process is clear: 'Academy trials will last a period of approximately six weeks, during which time the player will train and play with the current registered players in the relevant age group, monitored by the Academy staff.'[7]

At Motherwell, like Hearts, their process involves being invited in for a trial period with their relevant academy squad. 'If the trial goes well and the player impresses the Academy Coaching and Recruitment staff then he will be offered a Pro Youth contract and join the Academy squad.'[8] This is a perfectly normal process and one that will differ little from club to club.

However, it's likely that it will be difficult to impress the decision-makers when comparisons are being made to those who have accumulated the previously discussed advantages. What it does, however, is positively reinforce that the initial selections were the correct ones. I've often heard it said that 'there's just no way that what's out there is better than what we've already got'. I've taken young players to elite academy trials, and I too got that impression from watching what I was seeing. The level of intensity, competitiveness and confidence among those already in the system is striking. They wouldn't be there if, as a minimum, they didn't have these type of traits.

Naturally enough then, if you're going to an enter the academy system, after the initial 'early' selection point, for the best part you would need to be at least as good as what's already there, but you need to have done it without all the additional resources and expertise that those in System 1 have received – the odds aren't in your favour. By way of contrast, when the Forth Valley Football Academy ceased to function in December 2017, it's believed that a high percentage of the players who were released were re-signed by CAS teams soon after. Again, the belief and evidence would suggest that the talent is already in the elite system – the vicious circle of being 'stuck' in System 2 carries on.

Why is this a problem? These types of comparisons have driven a perception that that there's simply a lack of quality and no strength in depth. Not only that, but such early comparisons have led some to the conclusion that not only is there not 'better out there' but there's also too many in 'here'. This has a driven arguments for reducing the size of our elite talent pools further. In 2017, and to bring about an even greater focus on talent development, Project Brave proposed that the number of funded academies should be cut from 29 to 16, which would streamline the number of players in the academy system from 2,500 to around 1,200.[9] This strongly relies on the belief that we're able to spot and then develop the 'talent' over a period of many years, a belief and approach that continues to be the key defining feature of the system for player development throughout this century.

With every new decade, and with another generation of players not meeting the required standard, we seem to double down on the concept of talent and our ability to select it. The strategy in Scotland is clear: whether its 1,000 or 3,000, it's a *belief in small numbers game* and, for some, the smaller the better.

Historical perspective

Not that much has changed from the way things were done in the 20th century; however, there are subtle and significant differences. At face value, the world of TI wasn't that different. Scouts and scouting networks were commonplace. Talent hotbeds were well known. There was bang for your buck to be had in Scotland and everyone knew it. The same is true today. There's no doubt about it, there's talent in Scotland, whether in the elite system or not, and everyone knows it. According to former Sheffield Wednesday boss Darren Moore, 'We've always had strong links up in Scotland, we've got things up north really covered – we've got our finger on the pulse in terms of players, because it is a hotbed of talent up there.'[10]

He's not the only one keeping tabs on Scotland's talent. Liverpool recently signed 16-year-old winger Ben Doak from Celtic, who had been there from a young age and had progressed through their school's partnership with St Ninian's. Meanwhile, 17-year-old Kerr Smith, who had been with Dundee United since the age of ten, was recruited to join Aston Villa's academy. Further afield, 16-year-old Liam Morrison joined Bayern Munich, the former Celtic youth player signing a three-year deal with the German giants in 2019.

Cross-border scouting networks have been commonplace for some time, and they circle around the known hotbeds. One such hotbed was Possil YM in Glasgow, who would go on to become a feeder club for English clubs such as

Arsenal, Sunderland and Coventry. This hotbed of football talent is said to owe much to the legendary Bobby Dinnie. He played for the club in the 50s before going on to become manager while still in his 20s. His first encounter with Arsenal is told in his memoirs, *The Scout: The Bobby Dinnie Story*:

> One Saturday, Arsenal's chief scout came to see us, I didn't know who he was at the time, but he was very impressed with some of our boys. He came back to see us on the Monday night and said his name was Joe Hill and that he would like to fly six of the boys down to Arsenal and take me with them. That's how our association with Arsenal started. Some of the players went on to do very well at Highbury, like Eddie Kelly, who was part of their team that won the league and cup double in 1971.[11]

According to Sir Alex Ferguson, Dinnie had an ability to spot talent and then nurture them to greater things, most notably Kenny Dalglish. Prior to signing for Celtic, Dalglish had played for Possil YM and Glasgow United before leaving school at 15 to work in a joinery business close to his house. This would allow him to work during the day and train at night. Dalglish caught the eye of Celtic when they wanted a match against his boys' club. According to Dalglish, it was because 'two or three of the boys had become apprentices at Celtic so they asked if we could play them'.[12] While Dalglish would find fame with Celtic, other Possil graduates include former Rangers favourites such as Alex Forsyth, Bobby Russell, Robert Fleck and Gary McSwegan.[13]

In many ways Dinnie captures a key part of The System in Scottish football that's still intact today, where an influential and well-respected individual can be a gatekeeper to progression in the game. They have a trusted eye and are taken seriously when they make a recommendation. All regions have them. Jim Baxter grew up in Hill of Beath where his talent was spotted by Crossgates Primrose scout Willie Butchart. Baxter was spotted by Butchart as a 'skinny 15-year-old' and signed him for Primrose. Baxter left school and spent eight months as an apprentice cabinet maker. In 1957, at the age of 17, he was signed by Raith Rovers and supplemented his part-time reserve-team wages by working as a coal miner. He then moved to Rangers in June 1960 and by August of the same year made his first-team debut.[14]

Like Baxter, Scott Brown would also tread the path from Hill of Beath to professional football, but this time to the other side of the Old Firm. The town still has a real footballing fervour to it. The local age-group team Blue Brazil, in Cowdenbeath (taking its name from the nickname of the local professional team), is one of Fife's most 'scouted' from clubs.[15] In Edinburgh, Hutchison Vale Football Club is famed for its track record in bringing players through its set-up into the professional game. Based in the Saughton area of the city, they currently have between 400 and 500 boys and girls playing across 20 different teams. The club boasts more than 30 full Scottish internationals among its alumni, including the likes of Leigh Griffiths, Allan McGregor, John Collins, Michael Stewart, Kenny Miller and Kevin Thomson, among others.[16] Footballing hotbeds still exist, mainly concentrated in the west of Scotland, as shown in the following table:

League appearances by local council of birth across all cinch competitions 2022 (Source: Andrew Caskie @ caskieandrew)

Local Council Area	Appearances
Glasgow City	548
North Lanarkshire	380
City of Edinburgh	329
South Lanarkshire	167
West Lothian	162
Aberdeen City	148
Dundee City	111
Aberdeenshire	111
Fife	91
North Ayrshire	78
Perth and Kinross	77
Stirling	69

While the selection process of the past appears to be much the same as today, there is in fact a key difference, and it's significant. Perhaps you've spotted it for yourself? No? This time it's not just the later entry point into the elite pathway that characterised the 20th century, although that's a big part of it and shouldn't be lost on us. It's an important recurring theme: if you're a Baxter, Dalglish or Collins and you're 15, and it's the year 2023 in Scotland, then the window is closing on you. I can only imagine how Baxter, a skinny 15-year-old, would have been perceived by a CAS scout as a nine-year-old in a U10 trial featuring early-specialised and motivated millennials.

The theme that most strikes me is the role of the grassroots in the development of these players, and what the CAS structure has done to this. McLeish clearly highlighted this among the weaknesses of the current set-up of the grassroots, youth and recreational game, which:

> lacks any real sense of a national or collective mindset dedicated to talent recognition and development [...] We are not tapping the potential and as a consequence there is a talent gap between the youth development at grass-root levels and the performance and quality of players coming through to national and club level.[17]

This collective mindset existed previously. Collins signed for Hibs and immediately went back to his boys' club for six months. Before then, at 15, Collins, was told at Dundee United that he had 'not quite got it' and that he was too small and a bit weak. A month after the trial with United and determined to prove them wrong, he went on trial at Hibs where Pat Stanton offered him a deal. The following year, at 16, he used the time at his boys' club to, as Collins recalls, '[train] every day like a beast, I was in the gym trying to build my 9-stone frame up, the season finished and I'll never forget my dad says, you don't stop training, you're going back pre-season to be the fittest at that training ground'.[18] He would go on to make his first-team debut at 17.

If we get the developmental conditions right, things can move quickly. In the development of players in the last century there appears to be a closer connection with the grassroots than there is today. Undoubtedly Collins benefited from being able to continue to play for his boys' club, and they benefited from having him back, particularly his team-mates, who could then benchmark themselves against him to raise their own standards and could see a pathway into the professional game. It's a pathway that not only stays 'open', but also one that reflects a more collective mindset in relation to youth development and players coming through to play club and national football.

This collective mindset was the prevailing culture at the time. After signing for Celtic, Dalglish was farmed out to Cumbernauld United, where he continued to work as an apprentice joiner while playing for them. Dalglish attributes some of his success to this experience. Again, it was a move that benefited not only Dalglish but those around him.[19]

Contrast this with a 15- or 16-year-old playing in best vs best cross-academy fixtures, and we can see a clear cultural difference in the environmental conditions of the development of players spanning across the two centuries. The connection with the grassroots game has been a major concern since the predecessor to CAS, the Youth Football Initiative, was set up in 1995/96. Not only were there concerns that in some areas boys' teams were being decimated by players being picked up by the pro-youth system, but those also playing in the 'performance' programme could only play for their senior clubs as they were deemed to be the 'cream of the crop' and, as such, the senior clubs would assume responsibility for their education and development.

Many issues in this area continue to persist today, and they are to the detriment of the grassroots game, while doing little or nothing by way of creating the conditions for the development of better players. While much development has gone into the grassroots game, which can be seen in the investment of facilities and coach education, more needs to be done in relation to how Systems 1 and 2 meaningfully interact for the benefit of all.

An eye for a player

Statistics would suggest that, over a 30-year period, the quality and quantity of players needed to elevate our game weren't in the system. The question for the moment is: if you ignore statistics when thinking about TI and the probability of a player being plucked from a boys' team and becoming a world-class player, then what type of reasoning are you using to make these decisions and judgments? These questions lead us on to the ground-breaking work of psychology professors Daniel Kahneman and Amos Tversky. Their intellectual collaborations are profound to the extent that they impact all our lives. They've revolutionised everything from medicine to finance, how we're governed and also the world of sport. Principally, they've shed light on how the mind errs when forced to make decisions about uncertain situations, and they called this 'heuristics'.[20]

One of their first contributions on making judgements and how we make decisions was called 'subjective probability'. This is simply the odds you're assigning to something when you're essentially guessing. When it comes to TI, it's a type of 'what are the odds of this player making it versus that player?' If the odds seem greater that one player is going to make it, then the selection problem has been narrowed down – and so it continues. Subjective probability is the decision-making process that's assigned to uncertain events, such as the likelihood of a ten-year-old turning into a professional footballer; a ten-year-old turning into the next Lionel Messi; a ten-year-old Messi turning into the next Maradona; or a ten-year-old simply not having what it takes. But what are we basing these judgements on?

According to Kahneman and Tversky, we make these judgements by comparing what we're seeing to a mental model we have in our mind. When it comes to football, it's fairly obvious how we construct mental models. It involves a judgement about how closely the child represents the characteristics of the adult performer. This can lead to predictions in relation to how we see the potential of the individual. When we see a young player with drive, intensity, strength, competitiveness and good basic technique, we see someone modelling the future desired state – they appear to have the characteristics needed to 'play' the game at a high level.

These young people have modelled enough key characteristics to differentiate themselves from those who don't match the model. We may have several different models. When we see a 13-year-old Karamoko Dembélé, we judge his potential against a different mental model, Dembélé was labelled a 'wonderkid' and regularly talked about as having Messi-like qualities – again his potential was being judged on a future desired state based, on what we saw in the here and now.

This mental model goes beyond the way we judge children, as it can also lead to the modelling of the world around the child to further reflect the characteristics of the desired outcome. This can take the form of the structure of commercial coaching academies that model the elite structure, beliefs about 'extra' training, diet and nutrition, and more superficial things such as having the latest boots or carrying yourself like a professional. This reinforces the notion of mental models and decision-making in youth football.

Research indicates that when it comes to identifying who we believe to be the most talented children, a lay person with little knowledge of a sport is only slightly less effective than an expert at predicting who will go on to be a high achiever in a sport. The problem with selection at a young age is that it's not difficult to turn up at your local park and spot the best eight-, nine- or ten-year-olds. For several reasons the best children at this age are easy to spot. So-called 'talented' youngsters are what Rasmus Ankersen, author of *The Gold Mine Effect*, describes as the 'screaming talent'.[21] The talent that literally can't be missed. However, it's a lot more difficult to spot, or have confidence in selecting, what Ankersen describes as the 'whispering talent', those who don't quite stand out, those who tick fewer boxes than the screaming talent.

It's an easy concept to test. If you think you have a good eye for a player, try this experiment. Take someone who knows nothing about football to a U10 match. If you can, make it one where you don't know the players. Ask them to identify the two or three best players from both teams and see if you agree with them. If they can only spot one, did you agree? If they couldn't spot any, did you agree? When they did identify what they believed to be the best players, what reason did they give? What qualities did they believe the players possessed? Again, did you agree?

Furthermore, when it comes to selecting talent, you're trying to make a prediction ten years into the future. There are many 'basic' flaws inherent in this issue. Not only do we not know what the child will be like in ten years' time, but we don't even know what the demands of the game will be like. Our 'champions model' Barcelona team of 2008/09 dominated football with what was a physically diminutive team, as mentioned previously.

As the model changes so can what a team are 'looking' for, change. Then there's the issue of the playing style and playing philosophy the team has. Every top-level coach has a playing philosophy, the way they see the game, the way they want to play the game. It's not uncommon to hear a manager say 'This is the way I see the game' and it's important that all age groups are following this model. The theory here is that the academy system will produce first-team-ready players familiar with both system and philosophy and, as such, the characteristics to do so. This approach is flawed on many levels: coaches leave and new coaches come in with new philosophies. This puts many clubs in a regular state of flux and transition.

In 2009, Andy Robertson was released by Celtic at 15 years of age, as he was deemed to be too small. In 2017 he told the *Liverpool Echo*:

> There was a transition going on at Celtic at the time where a new head of youth (Chris McCart) had come in. I didn't fit his bill. He came from Motherwell who were full of big lads and were

physical. That wasn't my game. I was small. I'm not big now but it took me time to grow and fill out. He saw a small guy playing centre mid, left mid or left-back at that time who was quite weak.[22]

Robertson found a home in third-tier football with Queen's Park before moving to Dundee United in 2013. Eventually, after a spell at Hull City, Jürgen Klopp signed him for Liverpool for around £8m. Eight years after being released by Celtic, Robertson is regarded as one of the best full-backs in the world, known for his power and athleticism.

So where are we now?

The country has been covered and the screaming talent has been brought in, and that's only right. If, under the current set-up, the decision must be screaming talent versus whispering talent, then there's only one justifiable choice to make, as there's just not enough evidence to support any other. The hope is that from the tens of thousands playing the game, the next generation of world-class players is in this small elite group of 'selected' young people. Not just young people who will go on to play first-team football, but the type of talent that will elevate their club teams, and in doing so go on to elevate the nation. Let's not lose sight of this: the challenge isn't producing professional players, it's producing top-class players. For that to be the case, within this small group we need there to be the next Dalglish, Johnstone, Baxter, Souness, McCoist, McClair, Archibald, to name just a few.

Even though we now have better facilities than ever before – more qualified coaches, better coach education and more money spent on the talent – the system hasn't produced anywhere near this level of player with the frequency needed to change our game. However, we continue with the belief that within the *small number* of players scouted into the system these players have been found. The problem is that when you scout players at this stage, doing your job well means you've probably got it wrong. That's to say there's no argument that you have indeed found the best players for their age. At that moment in time, at 10, 11, 12 ... 15, 16, these are the best players in the country – but the problem isn't today, it's in ten years' time!

Why then do we make so many miscalculations and get it wrong so often when we make a judgement on a young person using our mental model? The answer according to Kahneman and Tversky is simple: these errors repeat themselves whenever people are asked to evaluate and make a judgement of anything with random components to it – and there's nothing more random than a child on their journey to adulthood or, for that matter, Scottish football!

Chapter 7

Getting in, staying in and making the grade

Random components

Whenever you turn up to watch a match at a local park, you're never turning up to watch players from the same age group competing against each other. You might think you are, why wouldn't you? What you're watching is children who were born in the same year and therefore have the same 'chronological' age – or so it would appear. However, as they progress from late childhood to early adolescence they're unlikely to share the same 'biological' age. It's also reasonable to suggest, for reasons that will become apparent, that when you watch the 'year-on-year' successful youth team thump a lesser team, you're watching an older team play a younger team. This is caused by the random components known as 'relative age' and 'biological maturation', and this makes TID a haphazard enterprise.

The implications of these random components have far-reaching implications for those involved in TID – therefore an understanding of this across all areas of The System has benefits for all involved. There's no downside to knowing this information. So powerful is this information is that it may be the singular most important part of this book. It connects the present to the past. It has the potential to explain why we produced so many world-class players in the (non) system of the 20th century and why we haven't produced any in The System of this century and what we can do about it.

The 'relative age effect' (RAE), put simply, describes the considerable advantage that children born early in the year enjoy over children born later in the year, and that advantage can be seen in their academic achievement, sport and in their emotional and social lives. A child born on 1 January is almost 12 months older than a child born on 31 December of the same year, which means that by the time both children reach ten years old the early-born child has already lived 10 per cent longer than the late-born. This means that if you're watching a match of players born in the same year, you're not watching players who are all the same (chronological) age.

In 2014, Scotland reached the final of the UEFA European U17 Championships. Of the outfield players born in 1997, 10 of the 16 were born in the first quarter of the year (see table overleaf). All in all, 12 of the 16 were born in the first half of the year, again showing a relative age bias to those born earlier in the calendar year. Recently, researchers looked at the data of more than 4,500 competitors in every youth U17 World Cup from 1997-2019. In all 12 tournaments a significant RAE bias was found in favour of those players born in the first three months of the year.[1] It's interesting to note that of the group that made up Scotland's team in the final of 2014, despite collectively making 350 appearances for Scotland at the various youth-level age groups, to date no player from the squad has been capped at a senior level.

Outfield players for Scotland, born in 1997, UEFA European U17 Championship team. Table highlights team at point of selection and current playing status.

Cammy Ballantyne *Dundee United/ Airdrieonians*	**Kyle Cameron** *Newcastle United/ Notts County*	**Craig Wighton** *Dundee/ Dunfermline*	**Jake Sheppard** *Reading/Hayes & Yeading*
Sam Wardrop *Celtic/ Airdrieonians*	**Joe Thomson** *Celtic/Larne*	**Steven Boyd** *Celtic/Inverness CT*	**Ryan Hardie** *Rangers/ Plymouth Argyle*
Tom Lang *Birmingham/ Raith Rovers*	**Aidan Nesbitt** *Celtic/Falkirk*	**Scott Wright** *Aberdeen/Rangers*	**Aidan McIlduff** *Celtic/without club*
Jack Breslin *Celtic/Petershill*	**Michael Kelly** *Aberdeen/ Eastleigh*	**Devlin MacKay** *Kilmarnock/ without club*	**Zak Jules** *Reading/ Fleetwood Town*

In 2020, researchers conducted a study to investigate whether RAE could be found when looking at players at various levels of Scottish football. They obtained the birth dates of 748 players in System 1 and 482 from System 2 across the U10–U17 age groups. They also looked at 261 Scottish professional soccer players. In the U12–U17 System 1 group, a significant bias towards players born in the first three months of the year was observed.[2] However, no bias was found in the System 2 players. These results suggest that the older you are within an age group, the greater chance you have of being selected into System 1. The largest RAE was found in the U17 age group, the year before transition into senior football, and yet no RAE was found in the professional players.

At the time of writing this book, the Barcelona 2008-born age group has two teams and 43 players listed on the www.fcbarcelona.es website.[3] Of the players listed, 30 of 43 were born in the first three months of the year and a further 11 born in the second three months. This means that 41 of 43 were born in the first six months of the year; as for the other two, they were both born in July. It doesn't matter where you look, time and time again you see this phenomenon to a lesser or greater degree. Researchers from Cardiff University found that of 32 teams competing in the 2014/15 UEFA Youth Champions League (the parallel competition for U19 teams), 30 teams had a significant relative age bias. In the case of Barcelona, Liverpool and Galatasaray, you were 20 times more likely to be recruited for their academies if you were born at the very start of the year versus the very end.[4]

These findings aren't a matter of coincidence, they're everywhere when you look at elite-level youth sport and where selection happens at a young age. So much so that it's possible to hypothesise that if the cut-off date for selection was 30 March instead of 31 December, then 70 per cent of those boys from the 2008 Barcelona teams would be swapped out with completely different names because they would go from being among the oldest in the year group to being the youngest; instead a completely different set of players would be experiencing the advantages of the Matthew Effect.

Moving the cut-off date under which a nation selects its age groups isn't likely to happen. As such, if you can't move the system then you might just have to move yourself – and that's exactly what Steven Lawrence (the father of the former Anderlecht and Wales player Jamie Lawrence) did, and in doing so he made his son four months older. Jamie had been a member of several academy teams growing up in England, but the August-born player soon found himself on the wrong side of the RAE, and around 2008 he was disappearing from the radar of professional teams. In 2007, Lawrence's wife took up a job in the Netherlands and Jamie and Stephen moved there soon after. In England the cut-off date for age-group football is 1 September, while in the Netherlands it's 1 January, so almost overnight Jamie became four months older.[5] Within one year of the move, Jamie had gone from a write-off in England to joining Ajax of Amsterdam, and before long he would sign for Belgian club Anderlecht.

There's little to suggest that at ten years old the early-born player is benefiting from any major physical advantage. It is, however, thought that this over-representation is more likely due to up to 12 months of more time learning. While you might think this isn't significant, it most certainly is. If two ten-year-olds started specialising in football on their fourth birthday, the early-born player has had more than 350 days available to them in which to play and practise. Now imagine if the later-born player doesn't start specialising until their fifth birthday – now the early-born/early-specialised child has double the play and practice

164

time. The early-born child who specialises earlier can use this time advantage to accrue more practice and time playing, leading to better tactical awareness and decision-making, more positive reinforcement, greater fitness and the motivation and confidence that this can bring.

Let's imagine this scenario in an education setting. On their fourth birthday the same two children start to study maths. They'll take a maths test when the late-born child turns five and a comparison will be made to see which one gets a maths scholarship to an elite school. They both study for one hour a day. Who do you think is more likely to perform best in the test? One child will appear to have 'what it takes' because they've shown exceptional potential in this activity. Let's just imagine that the parent of the early-born child is super involved and ups the study to two hours a day, employing a maths tutor, while the late-born parent feels that 30 minutes a day is plenty, so they decrease the study time. We know how they're going to compare in the test. One gets into the elite school and the other doesn't.

The RAE is a random component because you can't choose when you're born in the calendar year, unless your parents have carefully planned this for you. It becomes more random when we consider the infinite number of different ways the story above could be told. Perhaps the late-born child has their study hours upped and gets a tutor. However, for the best part, being born earlier in the year, and therefore chronologically older than others born later in your year group, is enough to gain you some initial advantages. This all may seem too much to consider when it comes to children's football, and for most it is. They're only kids after all! But this is football! This is TI in football!

This is about gaining the gold ticket into System 1! The bad news is that the point in the year a child is born is about to become the least of your worries. Puberty is about to kick in and everything is about to change again!

From the Scotch Professors to a Scottish professor

Bastiaan Riemersma, head of the Willem II Youth Academy, tells the story of Virgil van Dijk, a story of a boy who spent most of his time on the bench during his youth career at the Dutch team. To this day they have a document at the club from one of his appraisals, where his potential was assessed as 'maybe' being a player who could reach the second team at Willem II.[6] For most at Willem II, if you weren't a regular in the first team your future lay in the lower divisions. Somehow for Van Dijk it was the start of a journey to becoming one of the world's best players.

> I played in the academy of Willem II for 10 years. There was a period at Willem II when I was around 16 that I was on the verge of not going through to the next year of the academy. I was not good enough at all, I was on the bench a lot. In the summer I had a growth spurt and after that everything went really well. I had an injury in my groin because I was growing so much, but after that I made big steps.[7]

In 2008, at the age of 17, Van Dijk grew seven inches, and at the age of 18 he was scouted by Ronald Koeman's father Martin for FC Groningen and moved there on a free transfer. Van Dijk had 'whispering talent', good enough to be in and around a professional club but not the screaming talent that would lead anyone to predict the career he would go on to have. He was assessed by the reserve-team coach as having 'too many limitations' to make the grade.[8] As Van Dijk suggests, Willem II weren't planning on offering him a professional contract. His youth coach described him as a well-liked but occasionally a difficult kid – 'a real little rat'.

On 29 May 2011, three months before his 19th birthday, Van Dijk made his first competitive start for Groningen in the second leg of the final of the Europa League play-offs against ADO Den Haag. The season after, Van Dijk was a regular in the first team for Groningen and would soon outgrow the Eredivisie club. However, even at 21 he wasn't the preferred option for any Dutch club. Instead, as we know, Van Dijk would join Celtic, then Southampton, before becoming a Champions League winner at Liverpool. For Celtic it would have been less of a gamble than in the Netherlands, where there was more quality to choose from. Even when experts looked at the more mature form of the talent, they still weren't very good at spotting or predicting that he would go on to become the player he has.

In 2009, one of Van Dijk's future team-mates was suffering a similar rocky road to the top of the professional game. As I've mentioned, Andy Robertson was released by Celtic at 15 years of age, believing it to be due to his small size. The experience helped him become the player he now is, known for his power and athleticism. He would eventually begin his senior career with Queen's Park in 2019. Van Dijk and Robertson were the bedrock of the Liverpool team that won the Champions League versus Tottenham Hotspur. Both players, who only years before had been unfancied by big clubs, had less than illustrious youth careers.

Van Dijk and Robertson are both examples of late developers who just managed to stay in a System 1 set-up long enough for them to make their eventual breakthroughs. It's worth noting that there's an interconnection here between what's being observed and the RAE. Robertson was born in March 1994. It's likely that this early-year advantage helped him get into System 1, but as the years progressed it was becoming gradually more difficult to stay in it, and that's because something far more significant is playing out in the background and it's the most 'random, component' of them all when it comes to youth sport!

At Celtic, head of the academy Chris McCart explains that 'a lot of our young players are excellent maybe up until maybe the age of 12 or 13 then growth kicks in. You never know what it's going to deliver to our young player, again, their athleticism, their form struggles during that period.'[9] While the RAE at maximum can account for up to one year, when it comes to biological maturity the difference can be up to six years. While the RAE is a factor, particularly to get you into System 1, as the data suggests being early born is an advantage, the science tells us that the biological maturity is going to play a far bigger role as the child starts to age and progress through the age groups of youth football.

The man pioneering this breakthrough information in football just happens to be a Scotsman. Professor Sean Cumming grew up in Orkney. He's currently Professor of Sport and Exercise Sciences at the University of Bath, where, among other things, he supervises PhD students at the Lawn Tennis Association and British Gymnastics, as well as those who are currently doing work at Southampton FC, Bournemouth FC and Manchester United FC. The work of Professor Cumming and his colleagues over the last two decades has led to a breakthrough in our understanding in relation to maturation and athlete development.

Cumming doesn't claim credit for pioneering our understanding of biological maturity. He can, however, be credited for taking the knowledge and adding a social and psychological perspective to it. He has given it real-world application. Alongside his colleagues, he's prolific in testing the implications of growth and maturity on how young people are not only perceived and treated in the system, but also the views and opinions of the young people themselves.

There are many significant factors that Cumming and his colleagues encourage us to pay attention to. Firstly, the journey towards adulthood (known as puberty or maturation) needs to be viewed in terms of status, timing and tempo. *Status* is simply the status of the young person's maturation at the point you're conducting your observation,. *Timing* refers to the age they are when a specific maturation event occurs. This could be the time-point where height increases the most, known as peak height velocity (PHV). This is the final growth spurt in the young person's journey towards their eventual height high-point. Boys who mature early may attain PHV at around 11–12 years of age, while late-maturing boys may not experience it until 16–17 years. Whenever it occurs, boys experience rapid increases in height of between 7 and 14 centimetres per year, and gain around 9–10 kilograms in weight.[10] *Tempo* is the speed at which all this happens and is difficult to predict. For now, though, in relation to the discussion on scouting, we'll focus on maturational *status*.

Status, as discussed, is the young person's maturity at the point in time that you're watching them perform. It may therefore be the extent that they could be pre-pubertal, pubertal or post-pubertal. For those old enough, the mind is drawn to the U16s World Cup Final of 1989 against Saudi Arabia. On that day Scotland appeared to play a team of players at a far more advanced status of maturation than themselves. Voice change and facial hair are two indicators of maturation status; however, these are less observable in the younger age groups. Skeletal age is another well-established indicator of a young person's maturation status. Of relevance to this discussion is that two children of the same age can vary anything from between five to six years in skeletal age (a clinical method for assessing maturity status). This means that a group of players in the U13 age group could have a skeletal age of anywhere between 9 and 15 years.

In a youth football context, Cumming and colleagues estimate that these maturation biases start to emerge at around 12 years old.[11] This means that by the time you're watching a group of 14-year-olds they could be anywhere between 12 and 18 when it comes to biological maturity. It goes without saying that for some this presents a considerable advantage. Early-maturing adolescents tend to be taller, have leaner muscle mass and are stronger and more powerful than their late-maturing peers. Not surprisingly, Cumming and colleagues have found, across several studies, that early maturers perform more high-intensity actions, more frequent high-speed running distances and achieve peak speeds faster during matches than less mature opponents of the same age.

It's therefore not difficult to see the problem this presents a talent scout turning up to view a one-off performance assessment. Even across several performance observations the same qualities are likely to come to the fore, suggesting a level of consistency. These qualities are highly desirable. They could be interpreted to suggest a greater hunger or desire, that the child is competitive and has a will to win. And then there's the effect these advantages can have on less mature players around them. Perhaps it instigates a feeling of being inadequate or simply not good enough. Not to mention how this might also inflate the perceived technical abilities of the older boys, such as is associated with playing against younger opponents. It's easy to stand out if you're the oldest in the group.

Being an early-maturing boy, however, isn't without its challenges. The key challenge becomes when the individual is asked to go on a trial and is now likely to be grouped with others with a similar maturation status. At this point their physical advantages are equalised. What we have is a group who are closer in maturity. We've likely narrowed down the 12–18-year age dispersion in a group of 14-year-olds to something resembling much more of a 'like-for-like' group of individuals. Everyone is there because they've shown what appears to be an intensity, a drive, a competitiveness – they look hungry. All the qualities that were perhaps lacking in their overlooked, non-selected age-group peers.

At this point, now that physical gifts no longer account for perceived talent, the technical and tactical attributes of the individual need to come to the fore. The children who are asked to formally come into the academy can at this stage be characterised as the most technical and tactical of the most mature players in their age group. This doesn't mean they're the most technically gifted players across our 200,000 weekly performers or are those that have the greatest long-term potential in the game. But they'll soon know if their physicality and technical skills will see them enter System 1 and become one of our 2,500 elite pathway adolescents. As for the other 197,500 still in System 2 ... well, who knows. For the moment they're stuck in the lottery of physical maturity, just hoping that *timing* and *tempo* kicks in soon.

You may feel that I've entered too far into the land of fantasy here. Well, not so. Back to Professor Cumming and co., who examined the maturity status of 202 players in English Premier League (EPL) academies. They looked across the U9 to U16 age groups, where a bias towards early-maturing boys emerged by the time they got to the U12 age group. Worryingly, however, by the time they got to the 14- and 15-year-old players, none of them could be categorised as being late maturers.

These aren't isolated findings, as in a study of 293 Manchester United academy players and 179 players from the Middle East, researchers showed similar results. In these academies the results suggested that from U12 upwards there was a significant bias towards early-maturing individuals, rising to a twentyfold increase the older they looked.[12]

172

When it comes to the best-performing System 2 teams in Scotland, it stands to reason that the best of them is also dominated by early maturers. Empirical observation would suggest so, as physicality can still be observed to be a predominate factor for the top System 2 teams, while if you go down the league or leagues it would be hard to argue that you're not watching a group of young people at very different stages of maturity. There are some exceptional System 2 age groups in Scotland, particularly in my experience in the west of Scotland. I think I can say without fear of contradiction that these teams contain many early-maturing boys – 'the best of the rest' – those who, for whatever reason, didn't make the early cut into in System 1. But I bet if you looked at their birthdates you might find the reason there!

Final thought

To end this discussion on a high note for the late maturing who have managed to be selected into System 1, in a study of the 55 14-year-olds tracked over eight years, of those who went on to play in La Liga, the EPL, Bundesliga, Serie A, or Ligue 1, 60 per cent were late maturers, while only 12 per cent were made up of early maturers.[13] Similarly, despite there being a significant bias towards being born early in the year in the Scottish football data, no bias was found in the professional game. It might be that older or more physically mature players in System 1 need to prove they 'can't' play, while the less physically mature need to prove they 'can' play – and this would appear to create the conditions needed for something special to emerge.

This has come to be known as the 'underdog effect' that places these players at an advantage. As we've already heard, it drove John Collins to prove Dundee United wrong in relation to their assessment of him. Ronaldo was a small and slight child, to such an extent it was the motivating factor behind his now legendary work ethic and physique. Andy Robertson was too small for Celtic. He didn't represent Scotland internationally until U21 level, and by this time he had established himself as a first-team player at Dundee United. He was able to hang on there in youth football until he caught up physically and things started to even out – only then could his real potential be seen. One can only imagine how many of a similar potential didn't.

According to Professor Ross Tucker we should be delaying specialisation until adolescence, at which point a watershed moment happens in determining the physiology of the young person. Tucker suggests that, in an ideal world, selection wouldn't happen before 16 years of age and it's not until around the age of 19 that the physiological cards you were dealt early in life are fully known. At this point, and only at this point, are we seeing a level playing field.[14] Today, Robertson is Scotland's 12th-most capped player of all time and he's still only 29!

Chapter 8

Time to close the first-team pathway!

THE LAST part of this section deals with the most obvious issue when it comes to The System, that of the first-team pathway and the inability of our top clubs to develop their own talent on a consistent and repeatable basis. After all, football academies exist to produce first-team players. The academy is the system by which they can be moulded to the culture and ethos of the club, at the end of which it's hoped that there are players who can progress to the first team and enhance the senior playing squad.

To this extent, professional clubs, via their academy, promote a pathway all the way through to their first teams. According to Lee Johnson, the current manager of Hibernian, 'The real test of an Academy is how many players can come through to the First Team and stay through.'[1] When it comes to the current system, the biggest success stories in recent years are the likes of Kieran Tierney, and although neither Nathan Patterson nor Billy Gilmour stayed at Rangers to affect the first team, they're still considered to be successful products of the academy system.

In order to consider the role of academies in producing first-team players we need to first of all agree (or disagree) on what can be considered a 'product' of a club's academy. Where would you set your boundaries for this discussion? How long does a player need to have been in a club's academy before you can say they're a 'product' of it? How many first-team matches do they need to have played to be considered a successful product? What would constitute making a significant contribution to the first team? At what point can you really say that you were a 'player' at a club?

When it comes to time spent in a club's academy, we know that many clubs are starting the process from as young as five years old and have age-group teams from U10 onwards. We also know that the 'review' of Scottish football sets the timeline for player development at ten years. How long then do you need to spend in the academy to be a product of it? One, two three … ten years? I would argue that if you come into a club's youth academy at 16 or 17 years old and then make your debut a few years later, you're not a product of that club's youth system. I think it's more than reasonable, and reasonably generous, to suggest that if you spend a minimum of four years in the youth ranks and had joined the academy before the age of 16, you 'might' be considered to be a product of that club's system. Again, I would suggest that these boundaries are generous, but for the purposes of analysis and to progress this discussion let's go with that.

At what point then, after your first-team debut, can you be considered to have made a significant contribution to the club? If a player goes on to make more than 100 appearances for the first team, this is defined here as making a significant contribution to the club. These parameters are, of course, somewhat generous when you consider the many years of development that goes into reaching an elite level and what can really be called making a 'significant contribution'. Playing 100 matches would seem to a reasonable return for a club that has sunk considerable costs into developing a player over many years.

With the above criteria in mind then, let's look at some of our top clubs in relation to how many players made their debut this century and then went on to make a significant contribution to the first team. Kieran Tierney reached this milestone for Celtic at only 20 years old. However, no Scottish player since Tierney has repeated this feat at Celtic. Before him, four other players met the criteria: Stephen McManus, Callum McGregor, James Forrest and Aiden McGeady. Across the city at Rangers, Steven Smith meets the criteria as the only bona fide root-and-branch academy graduate to sign for the club and go on to make a notable contribution. The fact is that if you're Scottish and you want to play for Rangers or Celtic you have a far greater chance if you make the switch from another club. At Celtic, 11 other Scots with either a limited or no previous involvement with the youth academy have achieved this feat. Similarly at Rangers, 19 other Scots who didn't meet the criteria have made a notable impact this century. What connects these players is that, for the best part, they were able to cut their teeth and show their worth playing first-team football before making their move.

What then of the other Scottish teams? Using the available data and applying the previous criteria, only Zander Diamond, Andrew Considine, Peter Pawlett, Ryan

Jack and Scott McKenna appear to fall into the category at Aberdeen. Hibernian can point to Scott Brown, Steven Fletcher, Lewis Stevenson and Ryan Porteous. At Hearts, Jamie Walker, and Dundee United's Johnny Russell are the only graduates to fit the criteria. Undoubtedly, there will be other players who could have squeezed on to this list. This was compiled using the available data and therefore some of the data may be imprecise, and not all data was available; that is, exact dates at which a player joined an academy or exactly how long they were in it before progressing.

It should also be considered that some players move on because they get better deals elsewhere and they might have made a significant contribution had they stayed. It also needs to be acknowledged that hundreds of players have come through these systems and gone to play professional football somewhere else, some at a higher level but the majority at a lower level. Producing players for other teams isn't the principal purpose of an elite academy.

Regardless of whether we could argue that additional players should be on the list, it wouldn't be many more. The data suggests that only around 17 players who made their competitive debut since the turn of the century have gone on to play more than 100 matches after spending four years in these clubs' academy systems. These numbers are worrying in relation to the notion of a first-team pathway. The reality is that when Aberdeen, Celtic, Dundee United, Hearts, Hibernian and Rangers want to strengthen their squads, on most occasions they appear to find what they're looking for away from their academy systems. This draws into question the extent to which a player pathway into the first team meaningfully exits.

When it comes to the 21st-century pathway into professional football, I often wonder whether the following conversation, or a version of it, has taken place between a manager and chairman:

Manager: 'We need a new striker!'
Chair: 'That's great, we've got four in the B team!'
Manager: 'Ah, they're not quite ready yet.'
Chair: 'What do you mean? How can they not be ready? They've been here for ten years!'
Manager: 'Not my fault, I've only been here six months.'
Chair: 'I'll get my chequebook!'

Today, the progression into first-team football represents more of a broken pipeline than it does a 'pathway'. To illustrate, data compiled by Brown Ferguson (see table below), taken up to the World Cup in 2022/23, showed that out of the 12 Scottish Professional Football League (SPFL) clubs, only Motherwell started a match with, on average, more Scots (5.6) than foreign players. The lowest was Aberdeen with only 1.6 Scots in the starting line-up. The average across the whole of the 2021/22 season was 5.1. These figures aren't surprising and are unlikely to improve any time soon. According to Brown, who works for the Scottish Institute of Sport and is the current assistant manager at Stenhousemuir FC, we now have more non-Scots (>60 per cent) playing in the SPFL than we do Scots (<40 per cent). Out of the 110 summer signings made by clubs only 23 were Scottish. The picture is no better in the Scottish Championship, where out of the 84 players signed ahead of the 2022/23 season, only 38 were Scottish.

Average no. of Scots starting 2022/23 – up to the World Cup shutdown 2022

Ranking	Team	Scottish players in starting line-ups
1	Motherwell	5.6
2	Dundee United	5.5
3	Hibs	5.3
4	Hearts	5.2
5	Livingstone	5.2
6	St Johnstone	4.2
7	St Mirren	4.2
8	Kilmarnock	4.1
9	Ross County	3.8
10	Celtic	2.5
11	Rangers	2.2
12	Aberdeen	1.6

To put this into perspective, using this data, Aberdeen would need to play ten matches before 16 Scots have appeared in the starting line-up (out of the 110 available starting spots). When they beat Real Madrid in the final of the 1983 Cup Winners' Cup their 16-man matchday squad had 16 Scots in it. Dundee United beat Barcelona home and away in the quarter-finals of the UEFA Cup and started both matches with 11 Scots. Only Dave Bowman from their matchday squad wasn't born in Scotland; however, he grew up in Scotland, played for Salvesen Boys' Club in Edinburgh and represented Scotland as a full international. To indulge this point further, when Liverpool contested the 1984 European Cup Final, they had five Scots in their matchday squad. Again, like many times in our history,

Scotland weren't just providing high-quality players to the home market, we were also producing high-quality exports.

Today we have major problems when it comes to the concept of a pathway, and these problems mean that many potentially top-class players have almost certainly fallen through the cracks that the system has created.

Bosman broke the pipeline

Scotland's demise as a production line for talent can be traced back to the Bosman ruling that allowed out-of-contract players over the age of 23 to move freely within the European Community. Alongside the abolishment of the 3+2 rule that applied to its European club competitions, this meant when it came to fielding their strongest teams, clubs could easily sign players that were the 'finished' article from abroad rather than taking a chance on their youth players.

This would profoundly affect football clubs' signing strategies. The impact was quick. In England, during 1994/95, foreign players had started only 28.9 per cent of league matches. By 2003, under a decade since the rule had been abolished, that figure was edging close to doubling, to 57.6 per cent. By 2008, 63 per cent of players registered in England's top division weren't English.[2] To fully illustrate the magnitude of the Bosman ruling, consider this. On the opening weekend of the inaugural EPL competition in 1992 only 13 players in total came from outside the British Isles; on the opening weekend of the 2022 season, 17 came from Brazil alone![3]

Not long after the turn of the century, the effect of Bosman could be seen in the pressure that had been put on the financial health of Scottish clubs. A PwC report had suggested that the benchmark of wages to turnover for clubs should be 60 per cent; by the 2001/22 season, only Celtic came within the threshold at 58 per cent. According to the report, 5 out of our top 12 clubs were technically insolvent.[4] From a combined wage bill of £10.5 million in 1989 to £110 million in 2001 – a 957 per cent increase – shows the rate and speed at which our top clubs abandoned their faith in their youth development programmes. Not surprising, then, that since the turn of the century we've seen so few players progress through our top clubs' academy systems and make an impact on their first teams.

The remarkable difference between England and Scotland is that, despite the Bosman ruling coming in, it didn't negatively affect England's ability to produce top-class players in the way it did Scotland. In the early years post-Bosman, David Beckham, Steven Gerrard, Frank Lampard, Michael Owen, John Terry and Wayne Rooney were heralded as part of England's golden generation, and at the last World Cup in 2022, to name a few, there were Jude Bellingham, Phil Foden, Jack Grealish, Harry Kane, James Maddison, Marcus Rashford, Bukayo Saka and Raheem Sterling to demonstrate that there's still no shortage of talent south of the border.

When it comes to player development, the Bosman ruling has been a shock to The System in Scotland. It was a shock to systems across the footballing world, but the way you react and the decisions you make determine how big the impact will be. Add to this that, in the period spanning Bosman and ongoing, unlike Scotland, whose deal with Sky collapsed, English football has been awash with TV broadcasting money. Despite England topping the league for spending in the transfer market, they've managed to keep the talent pipeline of homegrown players open and flowing.

Policy and the production of players

If Bosman turned the lights off for the production line of top-level Scottish players, why did it not do the same in England and elsewhere in the world? One significant factor lies at the level of policy. Currently the SPFL's rules for competition state that 'the Company shall not directly or indirectly operate any Homegrown Players Rule, Salary Cap, Squad Cap or Under 21 Rule or any like or similar concept or criteria'. However, in 2010, England introduced its homegrown rule, meaning that currently in the EPL, a club can carry a squad of 25, out of which 17 can be non-homegrown. This means that the remaining eight must be homegrown. However, they don't have to be English, although they must have been on the books of a team affiliated to the FA for at least three years before their 21st birthday. They can also have an unlimited number of U21 players in the squad.

The new rule, according to Richard Scudamore (former Premier League Chief Executive), gives clubs 'an extra incentive to invest in youth and we also think one of the benefits of that will be that it will help the England team'[5] However, by 2013, and with no sign of the green shoots of progress, EPL clubs agreed to cooperate with a commission set up by the FA to improve the development of players available to England. The commission was set up by Greg Dyke as FA Chairman, who in his first major speech, set out his vision for the national team: 'I want to set the whole of English football two targets. The first is for the

England team to at least reach the semi-finals of the Euro Championship in 2020 and the second is for us to win the World Cup in 2022.'[6]

Of major concern to Dyke was that many of the English players in the EPL weren't international standard and that the talent pool was small and getting smaller. Dyke was happy with the progress that had been made on the development of facilities and the quality of coaching; however, of major concern to him was that England still had a serious problem in transitioning young players out of academies and into becoming first-team players. His major recommendation was that the number of non-homegrown players should be phased down to 13, meaning 12 players would now have to be homegrown.[7] While the EPL decided not to follow the recommendations of the commission's report, this highlights that the issue of policy is key to addressing this problem.

The EPL felt that restrictive quotas, among other things, would undermine the league's ability to attract global talent. Among the concerns of some clubs was that the bigger clubs would cherry-pick the best youngsters to add to their ability to buy the best talent – which would create more of an imbalance in the league. Despite rejecting the proposals, England reached the final of the 2020 European Championships, and were narrowly beaten in the 2022 World Cup quarter-finals by France. England didn't win the 2022 World Cup and they didn't implement Dyke's recommendations on homegrown players. If they had, who knows? However, the changes they did make in 2009/10 have had a significant effect on the development of English players and the progress of the national team.

The number of homegrown players required in a first-team squad has opened a need to fill these quotas – it has forced the hand of all EPL clubs. The result of this is that a pathway has emerged from the English Football League (EFL) to the EPL and on to the national team. Out of Gareth Southgate's 26-man World Cup squad, 23 came through an EFL academy, played in the EFL or had made their debut in an EFL competition. Notably, more than three-quarters of those playing in the EPL and EFL now qualify as homegrown players, and more significantly, English U21 players have played twice as many first-team minutes compared to a decade ago.[8]

First-team football and policy that forces the hand of the top clubs has opened a pathway to top-level football and it has created a production line of talent that doesn't look as if it will dry up anytime soon. Scudamore was correct, the rule changes did appear to help the England team. Perhaps England will win the World Cup, and in the not-too-distant future – let's see!

If policy has the ability to force the hand of the top clubs, to constrain them into rethinking how they consider integrating youth in their set-up, what then of the potential of this for Scotland? Rather surprisingly, Scotland seems to be running in the opposite direction when it comes to promoting homegrown players. Prior to the UK leaving the European Union, it was relatively easy for EU players to move to Scottish clubs, while non-EU players needed to obtain a Governing Body Endorsement via the SFA. So EU players have previously moved to Scottish clubs without needing complicated paperwork. If a player didn't meet the requirements, an exceptions panel ruled on the case.

Scottish clubs frequently used this route, including the 2021 summer transfer window; however, not long after, the UK Government announced that this was to be scrapped. As a result, the SFA and SPFL lobbied the Government on what they claimed to be damaging restrictions for clubs in Scotland. The Government relented and agreed that the exceptions panel could stay on a permanent basis and players could continue to be judged on a case-by-case basis. According to the SPFL Chief Executive Neil Doncaster:

> Given the significant number of overseas players who enhance our league [...] it was absolutely imperative that we were able to convince the UK Government to maintain the Exemptions Panel [...] failure to do so would have dramatically compromised the competitiveness of Scottish clubs, particularly when playing in European competitions [...] the alternative did not bear thinking about – and would have severely restricted the number of marquee players coming into our game, with disastrous financial consequences.'[9]

Many fans feel that Doncaster was protecting the interest of the Old Firm, as they appear to be the main beneficiaries of the process. When the governing bodies and/or the leagues either can't, or won't, make a change in policy to benefit the progression of homegrown youth players, what then? Well, then it comes down to the clubs to address the situation. It's in the national interest, the interest of the players and indeed the clubs to address this issue. The clubs themselves could choose to implement their own policies that embed a philosophy that commits a first-team manager to playing players who have come through The System. While England have at least introduced a policy to help this process, examples worldwide of a commitment to a homegrown system are few and far between; however, they do exist and their merits are worth considering further.

La filosofía

On 14 January 2023, Real Sociedad played Athletic Club Bilbao, and at one point in the match 21 players on the pitch were from the Basque Country, of which 19 had come through one of the two clubs' youth systems. This wasn't some random coincidence, rather a clearly stated decision to develop their own youth and play them in their first teams. For Real Sociedad (*la Real*), it stems from a commitment to look inside first. According to academy director Luki Iriarte, the process begins by trying to build youth teams where 80 per cent of the players come from Gipuzkoa, and 20 per cent, ideally, from the Basque provinces. This provides the foundations for a 60/40 balance at the professional level.[10]

This approach is a return to Real Sociedad's Basque-influenced philosophy after a traumatic break from tradition in the late 80s and early 90s. At the time it was felt that the Basque-only philosophy couldn't supply elite players to two teams. Athletic Bilbao had gained such a foothold in the region that *la Real* decided on a new strategy. In 1989, John Aldridge will forever be associated with their decision to start to sign foreign players again. Within a year, Aldridge was joined by Kevin Richardson and Dalian Atkinson.

Despite winning at Barcelona and Real Madrid, *la Real* finished 13th in the league and only three points above relegation. John Toshack returned as manager and that was it for Atkinson, Aldridge and Richardson.[11]

Gipuzkoa, Real Sociedad's province, has a population of 713,000 people. Today, one of the keys to *la Real*'s success is that they take players late, not early. They don't sign players before the U13 level, with most of the current squad joining between the U13 and U16 age groups. Yes, they run the risk of losing players to neighbouring professional clubs but Iriarte's message is clear: 'Stay in your environment, stay with your family, stay with your friends. And if you feel like you're ready to leave all of those behind then you can come to Real Sociedad.'[12]

Players in the first team, on average, have spent 12 years with the club. *La Real's* approach is refreshing and to no small extent rooted in what the science is telling us: later selection gives more predictable outcomes as maturity and other factors start to even out. But it doesn't stop there. The club encourages the local schools to work on a multisport approach with the children up until 12; if and when they're ready to leave their friends to come to the club, they know the child will have played handball, basketball and many other sports. Iriarte believes this gives *la Real* a more open-minded and flexible individual to work with.

What then of Athletic Club Bilbao? If *la Real* are philosophically aligned to producing homegrown players, and this alignment guides their thinking and actions, for Athletic it's this and more. Bilbao are the most well-known football club of the Basque region and have earned a reputation for their *la filosofía* recruitment strategy; that is, since the early 20th century they play with Basque-only players. With this restriction and the global nature of football, Bilbao have been called the world's 'last local football team'. At Athletic Bilbao they have a Basque-only hiring philosophy. Against the backdrop of the Bosman ruling in 1995, when all other clubs pivoted their recruitment strategies, Athletic essentially ran in the opposite direction. According to Juan Carlos Castillo:

> The club is ... projecting the idea that it has consciously chosen to reject the rules of the new age of football, which include the necessary competition for the best available players in the world. Athletic has decided to become a 'non-subject'... in the system of global football. The club chooses to form players through its system of youth teams and the recruiting of young talent from nearby towns.[13]

In rejecting the 'new age rules' of modern football, Athletic chose instead to stick with their age-old policy of signing Basque players only. After the 1911 Copa del Rey, and on being accused of fielding ineligible players, Athletic decided from then on they would have a Basque-only or 'formed locally' signing policy. This has resulted in 85 per cent of the first team being made up of academy graduates who, on average, have been in the Athletic 'system' for a minimum of seven years.[14] The academy itself, based in Lezama, a small town of 2,429 people in the province of Biscay, seems to be no different to any other academy you would find across Europe. It has the usual array of training pitches, gyms and medical rooms, the likes of which are commonplace across the world.

At Lezama they're not working towards aspirational goals, instead they work to a philosophy simply of competing with only homegrown players! This appears to be the only discernible difference in the academy. Like every other, they place a value on the person, their well-being and education, but it's in their philosophy that they differentiate themselves. It's a philosophy that unites fans, galvanised around an ancestral cause and identity. Athletic are the 'unicorn' club of world football, awash with cash in the bank and assets on the pitch.

In the last decade, Athletic have reached the final of the UEFA Europa League and the Copa del Rey twice; they've also flirted with relegation. However, alongside Real Madrid and Barcelona they're the only team never to have been relegated from the top tier of Spanish football, and they've done it with locally produced and Basque-only players. To put this into perspective, and to show what could be achieved with a clear philosophical strategy to develop and play homegrown players, this would be the equivalent of a team from the central belt in Scotland competing in one of the world's best leagues, while reaching European and domestic cup finals, and with millions of pounds in the bank.

Over the years there has been much debate on what it is to be Basque, and therefore what qualifies you to sign for Athletic. Where were they born? If born elsewhere, when did they move to the Basque Country? Are their parents Basque? Are they Basque 'enough'? Do they speak Basque? Today, you need to have been raised in the Basque Country, which consists of three provinces in France and four in Spain. This means that Athletic Bilbao need to find La Liga-level players in a region within a 50-mile radius from Bilbao and with a population of 2.5 million. Not only this, alongside *la Real*, the region has another three top-level clubs – Alavés, Eibar and Osasuna.

A homegrown approach, for a short period of time at least, heralded one of the greatest club teams of all time (perhaps the greatest). The Barcelona team of 2010 featured nine players who had come through the club's youth system. At one point during a match in 2012 against Levante all 11 players on the pitch were La Masia graduates. Pep Guardiola said at the time: 'It's not that Barcelona's youth system is better than that of Real Madrid, Atletico Madrid, Villarreal, or Espanyol; the difference is that here we put them in the first-team.'[15]

La Masia is Barcelona's youth academy, translating simply as 'the farmhouse'. Its reputation equals the level of its alumni, such as Guardiola himself, Messi, Iniesta, Fàbregas and Xavi. The media have described it as the 'fame academy' and a 'conveyor belt of talent'. Such was the faith in La Masia that Barcelona opened a new £9 million-pound state-of-the-art facility in 2011. There, players are assessed in the academy and have an individual programme, and they're screened for future weaknesses that might cause injury and impair their development. They've implemented what they call 'Masia 360°', which looks at everything holistically, involving coaches, physiotherapists, psychologists and doctors. The approach is different depending on the needs of the player. Nothing is left to chance – diet, hydration, vitamin supplements and blood tests to screen for risk factors such as chronic fatigue.[16]

It's now eight years since the Catalan giants won the premier cup competition, beating Juventus in the 2015 Champions League Final. Either side of the triumph against the Italians, Barça spent €343m on 15 new players.[15] In the eight-year spell since, they've only progressed past the quarter-finals on one occasion. When Liverpool embarrassingly dumped them out of the 2018/19 Champions League by turning around a 3-0 first-leg defeat, of the 14 players Barcelona used that night the most recent graduate of La Masia was Sergi Roberto, but he had made his debut as far back as 2010. Things got worse the following year, with an 8-2 defeat to Bayern Munich in the same competition. By 2021, the club's debt had risen to €1.3 billion, putting them across the stipulated 'salary limit', and they were blocked by the Spanish league from registering a host of players for the 2022/23 season.[17] The history books show that Barcelona succeed when the core of the team comes from La Masia.

Concluding thoughts

When a player progresses from the academy in to the first team, it's often said that this shows there's a 'pathway into the first team'. However, if a better player becomes available and has already proved themselves at first-team level, for some the pathway leads back to the academy and for many they're seldom seen again. In this sense it's not just the pathway into the first team that needs to be addressed, it's the 'pathway back out of the first team' that's as big an issue. To change this situation, we're going to need to revisit

McLeish's recommendation in the 'review' that recognised this and sought to address it. McLeish stared that:

> The Scottish FA should reward clubs for providing international players and increasing the proportion of young Scots who have come through the youth system into their first-team pools. Incentives should be developed, as part of the income distribution process within the game, for clubs to produce these home-grown first-team players. Developing home-grown talent is an important consideration for developing club and country.

Of all McLeish's recommendations that could have changed the face of our fortunes on the pitch, this one would have made the biggest impact. Despite implementing almost all the recommendations from the review, this one was never implemented. The pathway 'out of' the first team needs to be addressed. From a historical perspective, pre-Bosman, clubs had little choice, they had to progress players through the system and 'blood' them in the first team. This meant that, while part of their trade would be learned against men in the reserves, there was a real prospect that when they reached the first team they would be there for an extended period. All other clubs were doing the same, so in this respect it was a more even playing field.

Yes, there's a pathway into the first team in today's football, why wouldn't there be? The problem is that there's little incentive to 'develop' a player in the first team – too much at stake perhaps. Instead, as we can see from the data in the table earlier in this chapter, non-Scots are the preferred option in the SPFL. Perhaps it isn't a lack of faith and more born out of a sense of doing what's required to survive, prosper or continue to dominate. All clubs will have their own reasons, but what unites them is that 'learning' your trade in the first team isn't an opportunity afforded to most young players.

It's unlikely that clubs will adopt their own internal philosophy to constrain themselves to field a percentage of academy players, such as the example of Athletic Bilbao, even though I feel this would transform our game at all levels. McLeish's recommendations need to be urgently revisited. Clubs need to be incentivised to not only bring in a meaningful quota of academy players but to keep them there for long enough for them to learn to be a first-team player.

In this sense, the most meaningful thing we can do for the player pathway is not celebrate that there is a pathway into the first team, but instead celebrate that there isn't one out of it – at least for a while!

Chapter 9

Review and beyond

IF ANY single saying or sentiment captures the story of the 21st century so far, it's that we've fallen to the level of our systems rather than risen to the level of our goals and aspirations. Nowhere can this be seen more clearly than in the problems we're now facing. With the goal of returning Scotland to its former glories, a system was put in place to make sure that the 'talented', those with the gold dust qualities, had the focus and intensity on them fitting of their status. The truth is that the system was already largely in place well before the review of 2010.

In the 1995/96 season, the Scottish Youth Football Initiative, was introduced in a partnership between the SFA, the SPL and the SFL. On the face of it not all that much changed from a pathway point of view by comparison to the old system. The main change, however, would put the power back in the hands of clubs instead of the players. It would appear a key issue emerging from the old S-form system was that clubs didn't have enough control over the talent. Up to this point, players could move freely between clubs. For example, more control meant it wasn't as easy to try your hand in England. Previously there was more freedom, perhaps a factor in why so many players found a base in the south and had great careers at English clubs.

With the aim of fostering and developing the most talented young players, boys could now be signed earlier, binding them to the club. This change meant that not only was it difficult to move clubs because of registration issues, if a player did move, the costs of training the player would need to be reimbursed. Another key change came with a shift in the age range from 13–15 for S-form to eventually 11–16 in the 'initiative'. Clubs now could engage with and sign players far earlier than before. Clearly this put the power in the hands of the clubs, and the Scottish Government would later conclude about the 'initiative':

> However well-intentioned the changes that have been made, there remain some significant, systemic issues regarding the professional youth football system. These issues have the overall effect of weighting the system too far in favour of the professional clubs and leaving children and young people in the position where they can be disadvantaged in terms of the choices they may wish to make in terms of both their footballing ambitions and their other life choices.[1]

By 1999 it would seem to be clear that trouble was looming as something wasn't quite right in the world of youth development. Clubs, national associations and UEFA were growing concerned with the state of youth development and what was perceived as a lack of investment in youth football.

This would lead to the new UEFA club licensing scheme. Scotland was one of the first nations to be awarded the new licence in 2004 requiring clubs to have at least four youth teams between the age of 10 and 21, with a competitive games programme, and at least one U10 team.

The review of Scottish football conducted by McLeish didn't put today's system in place, instead it gave it an upgrade, rather than a radical overhaul, a refit, if you like, and a shift in mentality. It put in better facilities, created more coaches with better qualifications, added more playing and practice opportunities, engaged with specialists in areas such as fitness, diet and nutrition and helped create the national centre for football at Heriot-Watt University. It's now a better-resourced and professionalised system that suggests we're a modern and aspirational footballing nation.

The race to the bottom gathers speed!

With the subsequent changes in the requirements to be licensed, without which a team couldn't play European football, clubs now needed to have at least one U10 team – the focus on the 'talented' was getting younger. The problem here is that it can create a situation where those around a young person recognise the 'value of an early start', which can in turn fuel a move towards early specialisation in the hope that the young person will accrue experience and advantage that makes them stand out when compared to a player who either specialises later or is late to the game. As I've characterised, being good enough to be selected at nine requires several years of engagement beforehand.

The race to the bottom (RTB) and overvaluing the 'early start' has led to concerns that this has played a part in pushing the sport away from its working-class roots and pushed it upwards. Three socio-economic factors interplay to work against those from a working-class or lower-income background: 1) Selecting early into System 1 requires children typically to be transported to locations where academy football runs – multiple times per week; 2) early specialising children are propped up by costly extra coaching and related activities that are available to those who can afford it – the Matthew Effect has started; 3) the demise of street football and informal play – a natural player development system that no longer exists.

Regardless of whether the RTB and associated early specialisation works against low-income families or not, the interests of the young person aren't protected here. The pressure placed on body and mind resulting from early intense and frequent training can have negative consequences into adulthood. Up to 50 per cent of all sports-related overuse and burnout injuries in children are associated with sports specialisation.[2] Furthermore, these injuries may lead to a deterrent in relation to participation in future physical activity. Early specialisation is also associated with 'burnout syndrome', which affects a young person's mood and mentality.[3]

Small numbers and a path of separation

Policy and point of selection aside, the one thing that stands out more than any is our focus on small numbers and how this has created a segregated system for the benefit of the few. The focus and attention given to those in System 1 means it's unlikely that in any generation of the past has so much been spent on so few. The number of boys in System 1, as a percentage of the overall number playing (the talent pool), is small. This has created a narrow and 'early' entry point to the pathway and, as I've argued, not only drives early specialisation but attracts issues with young people on their journey to adulthood. This in turn creates errors in selection and development, leaving us with our *cognitive biases* to explain what seems to be the unexplainable – in other words, we're left scratching our heads as to why some do and some don't make the grade!

Those who do become players of the type who can elevate the national team are, unfortunately, 'outliers' as they're so far from the statistical norm that it can't be claimed that they're products of the elite system. As such, to continue in this vein of the narrow 'single' pathway of System 1 is to continue to have a 'belief in small numbers' that requires you to ignore statistical reasoning in favour of the subjective probability that your mental model of what a 'player' looks like, when hot-housed in an elite group, will turn into a top-class player. Ask yourself this: if every player was equally resourced in Scotland, over a period of years, would the outcome be different? Would the same players reach the professional game? Would we get a different outcome? Your answers will reveal much about your own belief about talent!

However, the fact remains that we're rooted to this single System 1 pathway approach to player development and that pathway is one of separation rather than the path of diversity. The characterisation of a single pathway is one that believes that the path is the 'winning formula'; our footballing fortunes are then dependent on this pathway working. History matters when it comes to such thinking.

An upgraded system on the back of the 'review' took the best bits of the past and attempted to make them better. The lineage of the single 'pathway' as the winning formula can be traced back to the last century when we had the system where players were noticed at school and could be signed on the S-form system before starting an apprenticeship at 16.

Under the S-form system, clubs could sign a maximum of 22 players between the ages of 13 and 15. For a lot of these players this would then feed them into reserve-team football and then into the first team of their clubs. Many have expressed the opinion that it's a system we should return to. According to Jim McInally, the former Peterhead manager who worked in Celtic's youth department:

> I'd go back to the basic roots of football when you had S-forms. School games were most important. When you got to 15 or 16, the club picked the best six or seven and put them on the ground staff. You were quickly integrated into the first team – training and playing reserve football.[4]

Today, by driving down the age of selection we've systematically reduced the number of players who can realistically enter the elite system. The elite system not only has to make these selection decisions at an early age, but there's also currently only so many youngsters that the system can accommodate. As such, I've tried to highlight the critical points in the evolution of The System in Scotland and the single path that has created the errors that are coded into it, and that if not addressed will continue to repeat themselves. The old system was open for longer, there wasn't as big a rush because policy hadn't driven the RTB at this stage. This benefited everyone, particularly the late developers.

In allowing large numbers to engage for longer, it created a more diverse developmental upbringing, and benefited hundreds of notable Scottish players who would have been lost to the game otherwise. Quite simply, their place in System 1 would have already been filled by those taking advantage of what the elite system has to offer. The 'cream' can only rise to the 'top' if the path to the top stays open for longer!

Policies have accumulated over the past three decades and have kept us locked into a System 1 single-pathway approach to player development. The problem with this 'single' path dependency is explained by Professor John McWhorter:

> Something that seems normal or inevitable today began with a choice that made sense at a particular time in the past but survived despite the eclipse of the justification for that choice, because once established, external factors discouraged going into reverse to try other alternatives.[5]

In the early stages of a path-dependent industry there's an allowance for some variety, but in the later stages there's only one path, until eventually that path is the only way, and by comparison to the past it's an inferior option.[6]

At its core, the System 1 player pathway hasn't changed much and has followed a lineage from S-form to where we are now. These are all characteristics that are associated with path dependency where you're historically wedded to an approach. It's what's otherwise known as X=Y thinking. In other words, if we identify the best young talent and give it the best possible opportunities (X), this gives us the best opportunity to produce great players again (Y). Only, as I've tried to outline in the book, humans don't develop like this and a lot can go wrong between X and Y; as such, you need to factor in an allowance for R, S, E & B, or any other random combination.

What was needed from the 'review' was significant change. Historically, however, we know that path dependency, such as System 1 and those used in most national sports programmes, aren't associated with models of 'change'.[7] The 'initiative' and subsequent UEFA licensing criteria were triggering events that set development along a particular path, and we're still on that path. When it comes to change, the concept of 'path generation' allows for a better discussion on how you create a system that enhances the potential for better performance and people outcomes. In such a way that when it comes to dealing with young people's potential, we need to recognise that we need to create multiple pathways and opportunities to succeed at the game.

The future history of player development in Scotland

Sections 1 and 2 have been an attempt to look more closely at the basic elements of the system of the past, through to the present. This was an attempt to show how I've arrived at the line of thought that make up the next section of the book. What follows, therefore, is an attempt to stay true to the aim of the book, which was to look at 'The System' for player development in Scotland and the collision between 'science and reason'. Section 3 continues in the same vein but this time it's applied to a reconceptualised, reimagined future for the game in Scotland – a future history of player development.

The next part of the book will look to the future and sketch out what a redesigned system might look like. It takes a problem/solution type of format. I've sketched out what I believe are problems to be addressed and the errors inherent in them. Errors that can start small but when they cascade through The System can create big issues. In proposing solutions, these again are nothing more than an entry point for debate. I hope that some will carry weight, but I'm equally happy to discuss the flaws in my own thinking – I'm sure there will be many. Perhaps there will be additional ideas that could enhance what's presented – I hope so. The one thing we can agree on, though, is that we need to leave self-interest to one side. We need to work on behalf of the individual and their best interests, and in doing that the best interests of club and country will be served.

Many of the ideas in the next section cross over and are interrelated; however, in order that each one can be taken on its own individual merit, they're presented separately. They're a collection of ideas and not necessarily meant to complement each other – but some do. Some might even contradict each other. Some of the discussions are underdeveloped and need more consideration. They're also not presented in a sequential manner or in order of priority or importance.

However, if we don't get the first-team pathway fixed, and the policy needed to go with this, change won't be as big as it could be. Likewise, if we can't come up with a solution to how to create players of the highest technical quality, at quantity, even if the policy means they'll more regularly play first-team football, the overall standard of the game won't be raised, and the policy won't stay in place. These two issues are, however, interconnected, and it's the interconnection we need to address. A kind of 'what came first' type of question ... the great player or the first-team football? The solution isn't simple!

Each problem/solution discussed is laid out in a similar way. Problems are briefly summarised and the solution follows. In presenting the solution I've tried to use examples and ideas to progress an informed discussion, how we might implement changes and what they might look like.

To bring this current section to a close and before we move into the final section of the book, we arrive at where we are 'today', with a player pathway that still isn't systematically producing the quality or quantity of players needed to elevate us at home and abroad. We've talked about systemic errors that we may need to address, the potentially flawed assumptions that may need to be challenged. This book itself needs to be challenged. In many people's eyes there will be errors of judgement and flawed assumptions throughout. The final section looks at how we address these errors and looks at the potential future history for The System of player development in Scotland!

Section 3 – Future

Chapter 10

Reversing the RTB and levelling the playing field

CURRENTLY, A late-maturing individual born in the fourth quarter of the year has almost zero chance of being selected into System 1. This creates an early error in the system where we systematically cut off the potential of many individuals. These late-maturing children may possess the type of ability that, when they catch up physically, outstrips the talents of those who have been in the system for many years. The old S-form system, by delaying selection, ensured that later-maturing boys, and others who fall through today's cracks, had time to catch up with their early-maturing peers. This, essentially, is what we saw in the system of the early 20th century where diminutive players such as Hughie Gallacher and 'wee' Alex James were initially deemed too small to play for their local junior team. However, the system was open later, which took away the need for early specialisation and meant that later-born or slow physical developers had time to catch up and overtake those who today would be in the system earlier and accruing all the associated advantages.

The danger with selecting so 'young' and giving the advantage to the earlier specialisers and early-maturing boys is that the game evolves to their competitive advantage and in doing so drowns out/dampens the more technical and skill-based players. However, if we delayed selection, by the time individuals are brought into the system they'll have accrued a wider range of diverse developmental experiences. This would create a better mix of physicality and skill and the emergence of players with greater levels of individuality in their playing characteristics, a quality that few disagree is currently missing from our system.

By delaying selection, we would create a new culture in youth football. This new culture would benefit both those who would normally be selected into System1 and those who would not. The early selected wouldn't have to negotiate many years of physical and mental intensity or the anxiety induced by the shadow of deselection and foreboding associated with new selections coming into their teams, the type of anxiety that has created the well-repeated aphorism among academy parents that the higher up the tree you start 'the more branches there are to it hit on the way down'. Simply put, the higher you start/rise, the longer it will take to hit the bottom and hopefully you'll find a branch and stay there rather than crashing out of the tree altogether. Hitting every branch on the way down isn't a healthy place for the individual or for society; for those not selected, there will no longer be a sense that the door has closed on a career in professional football if you haven't been picked up at 16.

Jamie Vardy was 23 before he entered professional football, while Frank McAvennie was 21 – these players and countless others would be lost to today's System 1. There's talent everywhere and it comes in all shapes and sizes. The talent hasn't gone away, it's just not all in the system. Unless anyone can provide a reasonably evidence-based rationale for why not, the key message for now should be, *No early selection! No early deselection! Keep the system open for all!*

Solutions

Innovation 1 – delay, delay, delay!

The first innovation in the system would be to put in place a situation where formal elite-level age-group football doesn't start until U17. As such, this would see an end to the RTB. In the place of the elite academy system we urgently need to create more pathways that are open and interrelated; in doing so this will hopefully discourage the current early specialisation model that's driven by those around the young person. In this sense the pathway into professional football will stay open for longer and systematically start to even out errors created by early selection, such as: the RAE, PHV, the Matthew Effect and the errors made when selecting by using 'subjective probability', not to mention the demotivation experienced by those who are largely locked out of System 1 and a career in professional football. These are known inefficiencies in today's system, and if they remain intact, then the patterns of behaviour and outcomes will also remain intact.

The timeline is important, as at 16 it's getting closer to the watershed moment of biological maturation. Young people at this stage aren't only physically beginning to level out, but they're also cognitively maturing and more able to choose the path they want to follow in life. Imagine a system in which at 16 the child gets to choose whether they want to follow an elite pathway or not. Sounds like a crazy idea, but perhaps not.

Take the case of Erling Haaland, for example.[1] Marius Johnsen, the former professional footballer, studied Haaland's journey into the professional game.[2] Among the most revealing characteristics were that he played until he was 16 for his mother club Byrne; his training group consisted of 40 players (including one girl) and not one of them dropped out before 16 years of age. Most significantly, they wanted to take care of as many as possible. According to Haaland's coach of ten years, Alf Ingve Berntsen, 'We did not select the 13-year-olds. Many do. I am a UEFA coach and have a background in physiology, but I can't see who will be the best. How then should less qualified coaches make such choices?'

As such, at 15, the players were given the choice to decide whether they wanted to train four times a week (specialist group) or twice a week (recreation group). The kids themselves made the choice. Six professionals came out of this group, including five national team players. Berntsen said of his system of player development: 'As many as possible, as long as possible, as best as possible.' There are clear merits to a system that keeps as many as possible playing the game for as long as possible and, as Berntsen suggests, we need to do so in the best possible environments. These subjects are returned to in more detail in Chapters 11 and 12.

Innovation 2 – levelling the playing field

Bio-banding

The reduction of talent wastage and prioritising appropriate conditions for development go hand in hand. This is an issue that hasn't been lost on professional clubs. Let's return to Professor Cumming and his group of researchers, who have been experimenting with re-categorising children according to their maturation status (biological age) rather than their actual age (chronological age). They've labelled this as bio-banding and are able to categorise adolescent players in connection with the timing of their growth spurts. Bio-banding has the principal objective of limiting as much as possible the effect of size and athleticism advantages associated with early maturers. On bio-banding Professor Cumming says:

> It doesn't serve as an alternative. It is something that can sit alongside age group competition. It's not either/or, we would not want to get rid of age groups because if you want to match kids on experience, social skills, cognitive skills, motor skills – all of those things will follow your age, but of course biological maturity doesn't. So, bio-banding offers another format in which you can group children, periodically, to challenge them in slightly different ways and the approach we have to talent in football is to group players by their maturity status.[3]

According to Cummings, because the formal elite system favours early-maturing boys, the late-maturing boys are being lost.

A further downside is that the early-maturing boys aren't being challenged in age-group competitions and this affects their overall development because they need to be challenged to succeed at the top level. Cummings argues that:

> They can rely too much on their physical abilities and they are naturally going to do that, they want to win, they want to perform well, they want to get selected so they're going to play to their strengths, and the problem is you spend all your time playing to your strengths, not developing the technical or psychological skills which are going to be necessary at the top level, then eventually when everyone catches up with you you're going to be lost in the system, and this was a big problem.

This lack of challenge eventually comes home to roost when the boys who the clubs had high expectations of simply don't make the grade; coasting through age-group football isn't the condition needed to develop the attributes to be an elite-level professional. Where you have huge variations in maturity within the same age group, it appears to serve no one – not enough challenge for the early maturers and too big a challenge to bridge for the late maturers.

Several clubs have experimented with bio-banding and put it to use in tournaments where players are grouped by maturity status. In a normal age-group match the difference between the youngest and the oldest can be 15 per cent, which in some instances could mean that some individuals are twice the weight of others, so they were selected in a way that shrunk the variances to around 5 per cent. As Cummings highlights, you're still going to get tall players and small players but you're not going to get the 'David versus Goliath' situation of physical differences. This means that to get matched up physically, the earlier-maturing boys play up, which means they no longer rely on their physical advantage. Furthermore, they're now playing against more experienced opponents. The theory here is that they now need to develop additional skills to get through these matches. These additional skills might be quicker reaction times, better awareness of time and space, or perhaps new tactical elements of the game. On the other side of things, the late-maturing boys, when matched up physically, have an opportunity to use their technical skills and show their ability to the coaches.

The result of these matches has been positive. Cumming reports that the early developers have largely reported a positive experience, recognising the challenge it places on the development of different skill sets and welcoming the opportunity to learn from older boys. As for the late-maturing boys, they've also had positive experiences. They recognised that it was less of a physical challenge, but this had given them the opportunity to command a match for a change. Rather than being the weak link they realised they needed to be leaders. As a result, they could get more involved and play more creatively. Coaches reported seeing a different side of players. Players who would often be stomped on during age-group matches were able to show the coaches something a bit different – on occasions this could be enough to keep players at the club longer.

What is clear, whether it's via bio-banding or by other means, we need to watch out for the double-whammy effect in youth football. The effect of potentially having a later-born, late-maturing youngster, technical or otherwise, who has virtually no chance of progressing in the current system. Then we have the equally distorting element of having an early-born, early-maturing boy. The problem here isn't just that they're likely to be among the 'dominators' in age-group competition – they may be highly gifted players – but they won't find the appropriate developmental challenges associated with higher-level football in matches where they can simply boss their opponents. In these matches tactical awareness or what's known as game intelligence is likely not required.

The key is to find the appropriate challenge point for each child, and this strongly suggests we need to embrace mixed-age groups. A challenge point is the 'point' just beyond your current capabilities, where your 'hand is forced' but not to the extent that it breaks your hand, but where to survive you need to learn new skills. For the mid- to later-maturing boys that 'challenge' point sits in the age group below, which can be problematic. Parents for the best part don't like this. Playing up is preferred as it seems to confirm some sort of superior ability.

Lewis Morgan, the former St Mirren and Celtic player, currently playing in Major League Soccer for New York Red Bulls, by his own admission was weak in a lot of physical areas as a youngster. In 2013 he was released by Rangers at around 15/16 years old, but not before playing down a year. For him, being told 'you're going to play down a year group, that just puts doubts in the mind of a 14/15-year-old, maybe you do lose a bit of confidence'.[4] Culturally, in Scotland, we're not quite ready for this. A shift in attitudes will be needed before this is accepted practice. Morgan signed for

St Mirren not long after being released and by the January transfer window of 2018 Brendan Rodgers would sign him for Celtic.

Playing against older boys is a story well told in Scottish football and beyond. There's example after example of this, including Morgan, who would play with his older brothers and his pals, who were told to 'go easy' on him. Culturally, we've appropriated this with the types of conditions children need to prepare them for senior football, and for some this is true; for others, they need longer and, as such, we need a system that's prepared to wait.

We might have to wait a while for these practices to be accepted. After all, I bet you've never heard a top player put their success down to ...

> I got to where I am today because I played down a level, it really helped me to develop my technique and all the non-physical elements of the game such as vision, awareness, teamwork – it really helped my confidence, and I knew I would catch up physically and overtake all those brutes who dominated my age group. If I'm honest, that's where I feel I developed the creativity that you see today. If I had stayed in my own age group, there's no way that would have happened, you just didn't have the time to develop these things, it was frantic all the time. Don't get me wrong, I wasn't playing with much younger kids, but it was enough to let these other things develop. (Said no one, ever.)

Or maybe the footballers of the past did experience these conditions but just didn't recognise it. The mind is immediately drawn to the street football and the parallels with bio-banding. Teams would be picked by captains. Older players would take on a nurturing role, coaching the lesser players through, keeping spirits up and providing encouragement, even protection, a sense of teamwork – a safe-to-fail environment. Teams were physically and technically balanced, matches never finished 33-0, or unevenly matched ones were quickly and strategically changed. It was in everyone's interest to keep all parties motivated. Drop-out was low but players could come and go. If you turned up where a match was taking place you would be instructed on which team to join, and it was always to add a sense of balance to the proceedings. When you played again the next day the dynamic would change. You could go from being the youngest in the group to being the oldest. Your role would change, and then again tomorrow another new dynamic. Not to mention the different playing spaces and playing surfaces where a match could break out.

One thing's for sure: for playing down a year or as part of a form of mixed-ability groups, culturally we'll need a big shift. For now, it comes with a stigma. If it becomes the cultural norm, it has the potential to revolutionise the development of players. This, as we'll come to discuss, has implications for how we not only think about equalising physical inequality in age-group games but how we might think about our approach to coaching. As it stands, we're left to consider how many good System 1 early-maturing players didn't develop the 'other' stuff to go with their physicality and how many late-maturing players were jettisoned for not having enough physicality. Oh, and spare a thought for all the System 2 players who had all the same developmental issues!

Chapter 11

The fallacy of small numbers and the cracks in the system

Filling the cracks in the German system

When Croatia knocked Germany out of the World Cup finals in 1998, the German FA finally realised that something wasn't quite right in their talent selection system. There had been widespread concern with the lack of talent coming through the German system for many years, with the usual sociological explanations being given as the reason, such as kids were too comfortable, had become soft, more interested in video games, or didn't have the fight or character to defend their positions against the influx of foreigners coming into the country post-Bosman (by 2000 50 per cent of players in the Bundesliga were non-German nationals).

In his book, *Das Reboot*, Raphael Honigstein tells the story of how Germany turned their fortunes around, culminating in their World Cup victory in 2014. According to Honigstein, in 1996, the then German national coach Bertie Vogts, sensing something wasn't quite right in

youth development in the country, urged the German
FA president Egidius Braun to do more to foster youth
development.[1] Vogts wanted to conduct additional sessions
for kids who weren't part of the main 'system', but it was
turned down, as the clubs didn't want interference from
the governing body.

When Vogts' plan was turned down, Braun called upon
Dietrich Weise to come up with a more viable one. Weise
was a former World Cup winner with Germany in 1974
and his work in youth development was well established.
He had unearthed the players who won West Germany's
first-ever youth international trophy, the Euros in 1981;
then in the same year he won the U20 World Cup. He also
coached the likes of Lothar Matthäus, Jürgen Klinsmann,
Thomas Berthold and Olaf Thon, who would go on to win
the 1990 World Cup.

Weise was managing the Liechtenstein national team,
but he answered the call to action from his native FA.
Alongside his assistant Ulf Schott, they conducted nine
months of research and came to two major conclusions.
Firstly, the talent hadn't 'gone away', they just hadn't got to
them, and the ones they had reached didn't spend enough
time on the ball. Secondly, they concluded that if you didn't
play for one of the professional clubs you simply 'fell through
the cracks'. There are clear parallels here from a Scottish
perspective, as we need to reflect on the likelihood that the
celebrated production line of talent of the 20th century can't
simply have dried up and that there are factors at play that
are within our power to rectify.

Weise wanted to get more support across the system,
particularly targeting 13–17-year-olds, recognising that

all youngsters needed good coaching, as those not in the professional system were having to rely on fathers and under-qualified coaches, which wasn't sufficient – according to Weise, 'Papa can't be the solution'!

Honigstein argues that Weise got the go-ahead for his plans after Germany's exit in the 1998 World Cup, and what followed would be the catalyst for a revolution in youth football. Initially, 121 regional centres were set up to provide 4,000 13–17-year-olds with two hours of technical coaching per week, and an additional 10,000 under 12s would also receive lessons. Not long after the turn of the century, the national network had risen to 366 locations, meaning that 600,000 'talents' would be exposed once a year to 1,300 FA coaches. According to Weise, when Joachim Löw's team won the World Cup in 2014, at least ten of the players involved would never have been found if the system hadn't increased its reach. One of those was Toni Kroos, who as Weise points out 'hails from a small place in Mecklenburg-Vorpommern. No one would have looked at him.'

There can be little doubt that the bigger you make your talent pool, the less likely you are to become susceptible to the selection errors previously discussed. The smaller you make your elite programme, the more you increase the likelihood that many potentially talented players will fall through the cracks. Every year that you persist with the same system, more fall through the cracks. A national talent programme that selects early, and selects only those believed to be of outstanding ability, stresses the system to such an extent that the 'crack' in the pipeline, and the talent wastage it causes, are of our own doing!

Multicultural French system

When it comes to profiting from successful talent development, France tops the league. The CIES Football Observatory reports that three French clubs, Lille (+€379m), Olympique Lyonnais (+€282m) and Monaco (+€215m), are at the top of the rankings of the current big-five league teams with the most positive transfer balances since January 2013. Over the same period, compared to the French top leagues with a €350 million surplus, the EPL sits at the other end of the scale with a cumulated a transfer deficit of almost €9.5 billion.[2] Not the type of large numbers that you want to be dealing with. Of the big five leagues, a recent analysis of minutes played by players under the age of 20 by footballscience.net showed that six of the first ten clubs derive from France's Ligue 1.[3] Clearly there's a strong correlation between giving young players first-team playing time and their value on the transfer market. The issue of the 'first-team' pathway and its contribution to the current problems in Scotland has already been discussed and it remains the foremost issue that needs to be addressed.

So, what then of talent development in France? Again, it's a large-numbers enterprise with multiple entry points and opportunities. If the 1998 World Cup was the catalyst for Germany's youth football revolution, for France, after failing to qualify for the two previous finals, 1998 would see the fruits of their re-engineered talent development system bring about a victory on home soil.

In 1988, the French Football Federation opened INF (Institut national du football de) Clairefontaine. As well as Clairefontaine there are a further 12 national elite academies in and around France. England used Clairefontaine as the blueprint for the creation of their national centre, St George`s Park. Clairefontaine recruits from the Île-de-France region, which is the most densely populated area of France (and includes Paris). The Parisian suburbs are supplied with municipal sports facilities and are known for a culture of fast-paced informal matches, the type of unpredictable chaotic and messy environments that are known to develop high individuality, flair, technical skills and survival instincts that we might call guile. The type of environments that you might expect to develop a 'flow'-like state in individuals and, as such, the type of experience that would make playing on a perfectly manicured full-sized pitch seem easy by comparison.

The suburbs, or *les banlieues*, have harnessed some of France's greatest footballing talent – the likes of Zinedine Zidane and Kylian Mbappé, and France's success is testimony to diversity and multiculturalism. The World Cup victories of 1998 and 2018 are evidence of what these economically and socially neglected neighbourhoods have to offer. At Clairefontaine different cultures are blended with the infrastructure of state-of-the-art facilities. The mixing of cultural traits has created a high level of inner competition that has turned out be a highly developmental environment.[4]

In the two decades following the Second World War, immigration accounted for a 40 per cent growth in France's population and, with it, not only was there a requirement to address the housing crisis that created the suburbs, but from a football perspective it created a substantial growth in the talent pool and had a rejuvenating effect on French football.[5] According to Philippe Auclair:

> Thierry [Henry] was just one of many. What they
> brought with them was a certain insouciance, a
> love of fun, but also the mental toughness that
> is required to be your own man in the harsh
> environment of the banlieue – or the football
> academy, like the Clairefontaine.[6]

Clearly, Scotland's housing schemes were a rich environment
for talented footballers, and some have bemoaned the lack
of 'scheme boys' in today's academies. It's not within the
scope of this book to investigate this further, as data of
this nature is hard to come by. Obviously, this needs closer
attention as we look to rebuild and make sure the systems
are accessible for all. It's not enough that initiatives exist to
encourage sports participation in Scotland's council estates;
we need to make sure elite-level pathways continue to stay
open to all and aren't 'shut' by default of the structure of
our systems. In designing the system in the image of the
talented, this has created the early specialisation model
that has driven the pathway away from lower economic
status areas.

In relation to the growth of the talent pool and the
positive societal benefits of multiculturism and embracing
diversity, this needs more consideration in Scotland, a
subject we'll return to shortly.

Have academies killed Brazilian creativity?

When it comes to producing world-class footballers,
numbers matter. The bigger the numbers the better the
outcome. At the dawn of the Latin street football movement
there were 100 million adolescents growing up on the

streets of large cities. Two-fifths of those were reported to be in South America, mainly in Brazil.[7] In Brazil today, football, as we know, is embedded in everyday culture. It's estimated that the game is played by 58.9 per cent of young Brazilians.[8] To add to this, Brazil has around 300,000 registered futsal players, although as many as 20 million Brazilian men and women are thought to play the game informally. Futsal is an important part of South American culture and is played both formally and informally on small-sized courts, sometimes wooden and sometimes concrete (particularly empty basketball courts).

The game emerged out of the scarcity of football pitches in the 1930s. The last time Brazil won the World Cup, at no point in the final were there fewer than eight former futsal players on the pitch. Small-sized pitches are largely attributed as being a key factor in how comfortable South American players are in tight spaces, with little time on the ball. Futsal, of course, is a sport in its own right and is gaining in popularity in Scotland. For the most part, young people play it with the hope of becoming better at football, and for some it has also become a pathway into the professional game. In Fife one futsal academy has 200 children a week taking part in its sessions. According to their marketing, at the last count, 103 have progressed to professional academies, including Rangers, Celtic, Hearts, Hibs, Aberdeen and Dundee United.

Back to Brazil, more commonly today, by the age of 14, the best Brazilian players have been selected to play for a professional club. There they receive resources such as training, accommodation and an education. Much like other nations, the implementation of this system came on

Alex James, a genius with the ball at his feet, Arsenal's first bona fide icon, and arguably the Dennis Bergkamp of his day.

Hughie Gallacher, standing at 5ft 5in tall, considered by some to be the game's greatest centre-forward of all time. As youngsters, both Gallacher and James were rejected by their local team for being 'far too small'.

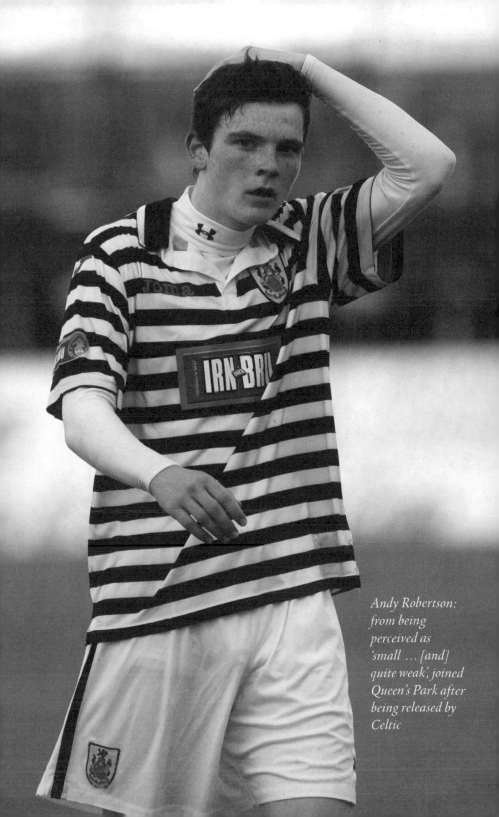

Andy Robertson: from being perceived as 'small ... [and] quite weak', joined Queen's Park after being released by Celtic

… to an athletic powerhouse and Champions League winner with Liverpool

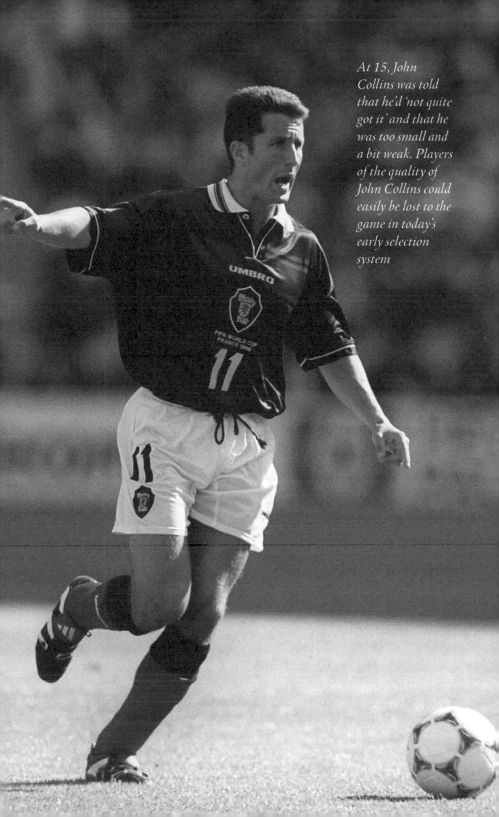

At 15, John Collins was told that he'd 'not quite got it' and that he was too small and a bit weak. Players of the quality of John Collins could easily be lost to the game in today's early selection system

Karamoko Dembélé was thrust into the limelight based on our 'mental model' of his Messi-like qualities.

Street football looks and feels like the real game. In many respects, street football was harder than the real game

… as with the street, red ash pitches made playing on grass feel easier.

Contrast the conditions of the street and red ash pitches to the development conditions of today's 4G pitches

The 'specificity' principle – if you want to get better at dribbling around cones whilst staring at the ground, practise dribbling around cones staring at the ground!

Creativity needs chaos – whether on the streets of Glasgow or Lagos in Nigeria – or anywhere for that matter – the conditions of your environment determine what you learn

What came first, the problem or the solution? A constraints-led approach involves creating appropriate problems, it's up to the children to come up with the solution.

the back of Brazil's crisis at the 1966 World Cup. They had gone into that tournament as favourites, having won the 1958 and 1962 tournaments, and would win it again in 1970. However, for numerous reasons, the '66 World Cup ended in Brazil failing to quality from their group. The decline was put down to lack of investment in youth development – sounds familiar. The new elite system was initially designed to maximise the potential of young players for the Brazilian teams, and in more recent times it has also become associated with the rewards for producing players for the international market.[9]

In 1970 Brazil won the World Cup again, their third victory in 12 years, coming so soon after the implementation of the new youth system that it's unlikely that it was down to this. More significantly, in the 52 years since, Brazil have gone on to win the tournament only two more times, in 1994 and 2002. It has been suggested that the academy system has driven the game away from its working-class roots, and similar patterns and inefficiencies associated with the systemisation of the game are evident. In an analysis of adolescent boys from Brazilian professional academies, researchers found no late-maturing boys in the U16 age group and only one at U12 level.[10]

It would seem that Brazil, when it comes to selecting for professional youth academies, is no different in having a bias towards early-maturing adolescents. To what extent Brazil is now paying the price for the systemisation of its youth structure is hard to tell. With a subconscious selection bias towards early-maturing adolescents, you invariably get an over-emphasis on speed and physicality, which can drown out superior skill and other key attributes.

Many feel this has been at the heart of Brazil s decline as a national team.

According to Zico: 'I'm sure that if I went for a trial at a football club today, I would be rejected for being thin and small. You don't see Romário-type forwards in the youth divisions, [the centre forward] is always a big guy. That's where the deterioration of Brazilian football begins.'[11]

It's highly possible that in driving youth development towards the professional clubs, they've fallen foul of many of the same errors that are evident in such systems around the world. No longer is Brazilian football so associated with the *malandros* type of player and the *ginga* style of football of the past great Brazilian teams. Brazil, however, is the epitome of 'the law of large numbers', and while the formal elite academy system may not be 'open' to all, the vast numbers means there are multiple opportunities and pathways into professional football.

Within the country there are 776 professional teams, 128 of them playing in one of the four main 'confederation' divisions (the CBF). They have football leagues in 26 states, plus the Federal District. Then you have the vast 'amateur' structure, not to mention the subculture of *futebol de várzea* that's played everywhere from freeways to favelas, which has played no small part in developing Brazilian superstars over the years.[12] In Brazil it's difficult enough to rise through the levels to play for your district or state, never mind your country. If you do, you've truly become something special, despite any formal development initiative, not because of it. Not surprisingly, Brazil produces more professional footballers than any other country in the world. According to FIFA, in 2020 that number was around 16,000 players worldwide.

When it comes to producing top footballers, the evidence always points back to one unifying theme of the *law of large numbers.* The population of a region or country is a significant factor. Barcelona is situated in the fifth-most populated part of the EU; Clairefontaine recruits from the most densely populated area of France; Ajax are situated in Amsterdam, which is the most populated area of the Netherlands. Around a million play football in the Netherlands (around one in every 16 of the population).[13] Most top Dutch clubs have a *jong* (young) team playing in one of the lower divisions – this system operates throughout Dutch professional football. Some play in the Tweede Divisie, which is the semi-professional third tier in the country. Some clubs have as many as 2,000 registered players – Excelsior Maassluis have 39 teams; VV Katwijk have 59; Quick Boys have 101.[14] The most successful amateur team is Ijsselmeervogels from the Dutch province of Utrecht; they alone have over 30 teams from the U8 to U20 age groups.

This creates a vast 'open' system of playing opportunities and progression into the professional game that we need to consider more strongly in Scotland. These countries are far more densely populated than Scotland and yet they recognise the need to work with greater numbers and have a system in place that's diverse and open. It stands to reason that a small country can only benefit from having the system open for as long as possible and by having diverse and interacting pathways into the professional game.

Final thoughts and innovations

When addressing the errors created by a 'belief in small numbers', we first need to accept and address the following:

- There's a generation of players who have been lost to the system, who may still be active, so we must re-engage with them – they've fallen through the cracks.
- Bolster your numbers and bolster them with more diversity. This will require a new approach and new collaborations, such as increasing opportunities for minority groups.
- There's a probability that you have future top-class players currently playing at a lower level who may never make it out of the vicious circle of System 2 – therefore accept that you need more players in your System 1 groups.
- Create multiple and interacting pathways.
- A functioning system requires 'as many as possible for as long as possible'.

It makes sense to follow a philosophy of 'as many as possible, for as long as possible' and we should aim to create the best possible environment for this to happen, Scotland should innovate the system and create multiple 'open' interacting pathways that can lead to a career in professional football. Such 'path generation' would need to continue to demonstrate that it can meet the UEFA Club Licensing System. Given the output problems associated with System 1, there would seem to be little that could be lost by drastically increasing the numbers in System 1 – literally, what do the clubs have to lose here? There are only upsides, for both the club and the individual!

The question then becomes: what sort of policies could be put into place to achieve higher numbers and multiple interacting pathways into the professional game? Not only for the purposes of producing more homegrown players into our system but because of the likelihood that many highly talented players are falling through the *cracks in the system*. How do we go about radically increasing the numbers in the system, the reach of the system and without increasing the financial burden on clubs?

In conjunction with the delayed selection into System 1, children could still have an engagement with professional clubs, and this would have benefits for all concerned. If children are going to engage, then the governing body should legislate to allow a player to spend a maximum of four months in academy football per year before the age of 16. In terms of statistical probability, it's likely that System 1 needs to increase its engagement with young people by around 800 to 1,000 per cent. An eight to tenfold increase in numbers isn't that difficult to achieve. This would mean an increase in academy exposure for young people from 2,500 annually to between 20,000 and 25,000. This will dramatically change the dynamic in young people and their physical health and will unearth a generation of talent that would have been lost to the game.

From the perspective of the professional clubs, these are the types of numbers needed to reverse the trend in the number of imported versus homegrown players playing in our top division. This not only has positive implications for playing standards but it also offers increased economic benefits, as in the long term it will reduce outgoings and increase incomings.

Innovation 1 – as many as possible for as long as possible!
If we are going to continue with age group football, here, for example, is a workable solution in relation to increasing the numbers involved with System 1. All age groups operate

a more open system. For example, U16 age-group players spend a maximum of four months in a professional team's youth academy per year. This would mean that every four months a new cohort of players comes in, meaning three changes of players per year. If at the same time you increase the number in each cohort, you quickly scale up the numbers and keep the system more open and less susceptible to the numerous errors previously discussed. This could be applied across all age groups.

If you were to have three cohorts per age group for four months at a time, for three blocks per year, it would mean that if you normally have 20 boys in an age-group team, you now have 60 for four months at a time. This would provide 180 boys per age group per year instead of 20, so quickly you've achieved a ninefold increase in your numbers. When not in the academy the player would return to their boys' team and play their football there before choosing whether to take up their four-month option the following year.

Multiple paths and path interaction should be encouraged. This would mean there's no need for the CAS best vs best system. In this respect all teams would play and compete in the same leagues – in many ways this would create a 'one system' nation. This would allow the professional teams to retain an exposure to players in their cohorts even when they're back playing at their boys' clubs. It would widen the competitive nature of these leagues, and the early-excelling young people, when playing with late developers, will help to bring these players 'on' – the sharks would be back on the streets, to the benefit of all.

Keeping young boys at their local clubs for longer has many merits. When Alex Ferguson took over at Aberdeen he disbanded the Aberdeen Boys' Club. According to Craig Brown, Ferguson phoned him to tell him he was disbanding it and he wanted to send him three boys he felt would 'do him at Clyde'.[15] At the time, Aberdeen were running four boys' clubs at all age groups, but Ferguson felt that they were too costly and at best they would be lucky to get two boys from them. Instead, he felt it would be best to send them to their local boys' clubs such as Dyce or Coulter, while the Glasgow boys would be sent to their local clubs and brought back to up to Aberdeen in the school holidays. For Brown, as fate would have it, one of the players was Ian Ferguson, who would go on to win 'nine in a row' with Rangers. Ironically, before joining Rangers, Ian Ferguson was on his way to sign for Ferguson at Manchester United.

This more 'open' system needs to be supported by a national mentality of doing what's good for the child and good for the country. If child and country aren't put first, then self-interest might prevent any real change taking place. Again, the evidence is weak, within the current set-up, to support any notion that clubs should continue to 'go it alone' when it comes to talent development. Taking a more national approach to developing talent might mean some further radical changes. We need to guard against the financially more powerful team's cherry-picking the best 16-year-olds. This might require something of a draft system to distribute the talent more evenly across the professional teams. The draft system is commonly used in North American sports to make them more competitive and financially equitable. Perhaps a wage cap or other measures could be considered to ensure that players aren't simply stockpiled at top clubs just in case they come good. Reducing talent wastage and the interests of the young person need to be put first.

Innovation 2 – Talent re-identification

Given that at least one, still active, generation of football players has been lost to the inefficiencies in System 1, it stands to reason to instigate a programme to re-engage with the generation of talent who may have been lost to the system. Football is a unique sport in that it metaphorically places players on the scrapheap before they even reach adulthood, and therefore this is also true for young adults. Many players have fallen through cracks via early deselection, late maturation, sociological issues and sometimes a combination of factors. A new initiative to offer all these players a route back into the game has many benefits for all involved and society.

Jamie Vardy was released by Sheffield Wednesday due to being too small, a month before a major growth spurt. He spent three years in Stocksbridge's second team in Sheffield's County Senior League, where he was electronically tagged after an assault charge. Vardy took until he was 23 years old to sign his first professional contract. He was still playing non-league football when, in the summer of 2012, at 25 he signed for Leicester.[16] While most academy kids are signed based on their physical and associated technical qualities, many sociological issues are playing out in the background of a young person (often issues we know little or nothing about until it's too late).

The longer the system stays open, and initially the more routes back into the game, the more all concerned stand to benefit. Real talent will potentially be rediscovered. It could also act as a positive catalyst both physically and sociologically for those, for whatever reason, who had obstacles in their way that prevented their progression at a younger age – who, if they 'knew then what they know now', would be in a better place to make the most of their abilities.

Perhaps within the elite structure criteria clubs should run 'shadow' teams made up of players who were never in System 1 or those who were in but were deselected or dropped out for other reasons. Notionally this could be open for any player of 25 or under. Initially this could involve running friendly tournaments before progressing into a league structure. Talent re-identification could happen through 'open' trial sessions. Scotland has many examples of top-class players who have come into professional football later, but in today's system these players would be lost to the game. This would keep the system 'open' for longer and have major benefits for all.

Innovation 3 – Asian professional football team
Numbers could also be increased by the creation of an additional professional team in Scotland. The question is, are the football authorities and clubs doing enough to engage with and encourage ethnic minorities into Scotland's national sport? Much like talent re-identification, beyond any benefit that this might bring on the football pitch, everyone stands to gain from a more 'open' system. Scotland has a long and proud association with generations of families from the Indian subcontinent. Despite this, very few have emerged from these communities to play senior football in Scotland.

Scotland's Asian communities make up around 2.7 per cent of the population. These numbers doubled in size between 2001 and 2011, representing around 141,000 people. This is split between 50,000 people who identified as 'Pakistani', 34,000 who identified as 'Chinese', 33,000 who identified as 'Indian', 4,000 who identified as 'Bangladeshi', and 21,000 who identified as 'Other'.[17]

According to Kuljit Randhawa, the Head of Diversity and Inclusion Strategy at the Premier League, racial stereotyping of Asians has acted as a barrier to not only the 'Asians in football' debate but more broadly the everyday lives of British Asians.[18] Misguided myths and stereotypes, such as inadequate physicality, the prioritisation of education over sporting endeavours and the perceived importance of cultural and religious traditions, have contributed to limited pathways and opportunities in the game for British Asians. The current highly gifted Asian players playing for Celtic can act as role models, not just in breaking down limiting racial stereotypes, but also for young Scottish Asians. Role models not only challenge the stereotypes that hold back communities, but they can also act as an 'I want to be like them' type of force that can ignite a spark in a young person.[19]

It has been noted that representation such as this should be made in consultation with the populations that it's attempting to represent. A recent investigation found that 86 per cent of the Pakistani-Scots surveyed from Greater Glasgow said they would support a new Asian/Muslim football club in Scotland.[20] Other initiatives such as Chelsea FC's 'Asian Star' provide British Asian youngsters the opportunity to showcase their talents in front of invited coaches and scouts.[21] Barriers, wherever they exist in Scottish football, should be broken down to make sure the pathway is open and easily accessible to all – particularly if it leads to a more diverse and multicultural Scottish footballing landscape.

There's nothing to suggest that an Asian professional team would have an Asian-only signing policy. That would be for the club and its representatives to decide. However, as with the example of Athletic Bilbao, there would be much to be gained on and off the pitch from such an approach. In relation to entry into the professional 'pyramid' system, now would be as good a time as any. Talks are currently afoot in relation to the creation of an additional tier within the structure, particularly as clubs are looking to bridge the talent development gap for their academy pathways. The so-called Conference League would seem to be a natural entry point and should be met with little opposition given the willingness to accommodate the youth development aspiration of our top clubs.

Chapter 12

The best possible environments

I'VE OBSERVED coaches working with youths at the Ciutat Esportiva, where all the FC Barcelona teams train – it's also home to the new La Masia – and they differ little from a session run by professionals in Scotland. I suspect you would find little difference anywhere you go in the world. Largely speaking, children will spend a similar amount of time on the ball, in similarly structured practice activities. Researchers have found that the developmental activities of elite soccer players aged under 16 from Brazil, England, France, Ghana, Mexico, Portugal and Sweden differ little in their approach to developing players.[1] While there were some differences between countries, typically they followed the same development route of early engagement and specialisation pathways. When it comes to the top footballing nations there appear to be no special approaches taken to the way players are developed that would suggest that it's the system that's creating the repeatable development of world-class players.

Despite this, we very often hear about an ex-player or new manager who has travelled the world to spend time at the world's best academies. The notion here is that this is where they'll find the missing ingredients. Graeme Souness tells the story of his time at Liverpool during their era of domestic and European domination:

> Time and time again [coaches] would turn up to Melwood [training ground] from all over the world with their clipboards and write down what we did. We would jog round the perimeter, stretch, do three-quarter sprints, break for five-a-side, a few more sprints, five-a-side, few more sprints, then go home. The [visiting coaches] would write all that down. By the third day the clipboard was sitting beside them. These guys would say to me: "Do you come back in the afternoon and do your real work." He thought we were hiding something from them.[2]

I can't imagine that coaches returning from Liverpool in the 70s and 80s really believed that if you want to win multiple European Cups then you just play lots of five-a-side football like Liverpool did; or truly believing that the 'rondo' (a drill where the player/s in the middle compete to win the ball back from the players on the outside circle) that Cruyff brought to Barcelona via Ajax was the genesis of Guardiola's tiki-taka style of football, and this is how you transform your team on the pitch.

This chapter is largely focused on exploring the activities and associated 'best environments' for player development further and, in doing so, attempting to apply science to reason to make my case. Centrally it's interested in the notion of 'best possible environment' and, as such, sketches out an argument and rationale for how this might look and how to create it. This includes the role of the coach and the coaching process but it's in no way an analysis of current practice within either System 1 or 2. Some will recognise aspects of what's discussed from either side of the fence.

Across the spectrum good coaching takes place, as well as some not so good. This chapter will discuss practices and ideas that will be familiar to some and completely alien to others. It mainly deals with what I would call modern thinking in the field of what's known as 'skill acquisition'. This is the field of trying to understand how people become good at something and how we can be put in place structures that complement this. It involves the role of the coach as well as the spaces and places where an activity takes place.

The best academy in the world

When you turn up to watch a professional team train, or watch the training at an elite-level academy, you assume you're getting an insight into the ingredients that go into making an elite-level footballer. As with the coaches turning up to watch the great Liverpool or Barcelona teams, or if you watch the cream of academy football at La Masia, you assume the same thing. The likelihood, however, is that you're watching players whose skills have been developed and honed elsewhere, and this is what led them into these elite teams. This is what Ted Kroeten, the co-founder of the free play initiative called *Joy of the People*, found when he brought in the youth coaches from Dinamo Zagreb.[3] The coaches were there to provide some coaching to the children in Kroeten's programme and offer some education for his coaches in the evening. Zagreb was rated as one of the top six academies in Europe. Kroeten reports that not only was it in the top six, but their coaches were also making the case that it was the world's finest from U6 all the way to U20.

One evening the coaches highlighted that Inter Milan had paid €17m for one of their academy products. The player was Mateo Kovačić. Kroeten and one of his colleagues were curious, because earlier the Zagreb coaches had been expounding about the extensive two-footed training they do. Kovačić, however, to their knowledge was predominately a one-footed player who looked more like a street player than an academy product. It turns out that Kovačić was recruited into their academy at around 14, but before then he played with a small local academy in Austria and every day he would play on the streets. At 16, and on his debut for Zagreb, he became the youngest goalscorer in the history of the Croatian football league.[4] A great achievement but a timeline that would suggest he couldn't be claimed to be a product of Zagreb's academy system.

Fast forward to 2018 and Croatia make the World Cup Final, validation perhaps of the claim of the best academy in the world. The system must work. So Kroeten decided to look at the data and there it was: six out of the starting eleven were indeed from the Zagreb academy; however, only one player had joined the academy before the age of 15. The list of players and the age they joined the academy is as follows: Domagoj Vida 22; Šime Vrsaljko 14; Dejan Lovren 15; Marcelo Brozović 20; Luka Modrić 16; Mario Mandžukić 21. Kroeten also notes that when you look at Zagreb's top ten transfers, only one player joined before the age of 15, prior to being sold on. Kroeten's key message is that you would think players who had been in the 'best academy' in the world from six years old would have an advantage, but the data doesn't suggest this.

There's seems to be no doubt that you don't not have to be in the best academy, or any academy for that matter, to develop the attributes needed to play the game at a high level.

Creating the best possible environment.

The 'review' of 2010 had made it clear that for Scotland to develop players of the highest skill level, a focus needs to be on the conditions needed for learning. According to McLeish:

> The skill level of Scottish players is well below that of other comparable countries and Leagues. Young Scots spend less time practicing [sic] with a ball than those in Portugal, France, Holland and Spain and the average hours per week developing technical skills, is much lower in Scotland.

It is, however, one thing to identify that we need to spend more time practising with the ball, but it's another fostering the conditions to make young people want to. As one notable educator puts it, it's the business of 'how to get people, often young people, to learn and master something that is long and challenging – and to enjoy it'. This is more relevant today than ever before, with much of children's experiences of football now in formal settings that place an adult at the centre of the recreation experience.

To this extent, who gets to decide what a session should look like? While the street is over-romanticised in the written and anecdotal history of Scottish football (this book is as guilty as any), if any statement captures what the street did, it's in the observation above that captures the pertinent conditions that it created in relation to player development. Wherever 'street' football was played, be it the street, beach or school playground, it was what we've now come to call a 'self-organised learning system' – crucially, it didn't require adult involvement – and it stimulated the interest of children to such an extent that the vast amount of practice hours needed to become good at an activity were easily accumulated by a young age.

In those days, typically, coaching was something that you received when you became good at something, but today coaching is the entry point for most kids. In the days of the 'street', motivation was driven by *relatedness*, *competence* and *autonomy*, which, according to self-determination theory (SDT), are the central conditions that keep people involved in something for long enough to become good at it. *Relatedness* simply means you identify with the people you're sharing the experience with; *competence* is your ability to do it; *autonomy* is the sense of the choice over what you're doing, when you do it and whether you do it at all.

The demise of the street and the advent of the commercialisation of kids' leisure time means that children are now introduced to sport via organised coaching classes and high levels of parental/adult involvement, and with organisation comes structure and expectation. Whether kids *relate* to others in the group is incidental as they're grouped together according to age and ability – meaning someone has already made a judgement about their *competence*, which, alongside the child being driven to the activity by an adult, has stripped them of any sense of *autonomy*. Undermining the conditions of SDT in this way has been shown to lead to negative outcomes and high levels of drop-out.[5]

However, when it comes to talking about creating environments that young people want, how do we know what they want? The answer is that we don't. What we can do, however, is observe what they do when they're free to choose. The most obvious place to start is to consider the norms of the computer game generation, and in doing so this brings to life the influential power of SDT in action.

Playing an Xbox, PlayStation or any other gaming device is closer to the conditions of street football today than organised football is. Kids game in communities but they choose which community they want to be part of, and this is usually a competency-based decision. They dip in and out when they want, age isn't a factor and they find their challenge point quickly. Much like the street, there's a strong self-organising process. When the streets closed, computer games picked up. Kids become highly skilled at gaming, yet experience little adult involvement and no coaching – when did you last sign your child up for an eight-week block of classes on how to improve at FIFA or GTA – let alone tell them they need to practise?

There appears to be only one other parallel to this in modern culture and it can be seen at your local skatepark. Kids of all ages participate in the same space in an activity that involves no need for adults, no coaches, and yet high volumes of participation hours are accumulated. Again, where the conditions of relatedness, competence and autonomy are met, just like on the street, just like with video games, something magical happens, and skilful behaviour is never very far away.

Kids don't need to be taught how to be skilful; we need to make sure we don't coach it out of them!

There's much to be learned about coaching children from observing their natural tendencies. If you give a bunch of kids an open space and a ball, a match will break out – no child has ever asked for some cones so that they can set up a drill! Perhaps in the future they will – let's hope not! Children the world over, given their own free will, would set up an activity that to the greatest extent possible would look and feel like the real thing.

Where over-coaching is happening, we need to guard against it. For that we need to know what it looks like! We need to know the impact it has on the child, their enjoyment and perhaps their long-term engagement with the game. The importance of the coach in the life of the young person can't be overstated. My son gave up his illustrious rugby career after six weeks of taking it up, aged eight, and when I asked him why he didn't want to do rugby any more, he replied, 'Because I just want to play rugby.' During the six weeks he had been going to rugby locally, inspired by watching a Scotland vs England Six Nations match on TV, he had done very little activity that actually looked like or felt like the real game. The game had been deconstructed to such an extent that it was unrecognisable to both participant and observer. Instead of game-like activity the sport was taught through a series of drills in the belief that they needed to learn the various technical components first before they could take part in a match.

The deconstruction of an activity can be thought of as a 'solution first, problem second' type of approach. In this approach kids are taught a series of techniques (the solution) and gradually they're introduced to the game (the problem). The brain has been separated from the body (in the sciences this is known as mind–body dualism) and kids are asked to run through various training drills in a repetitive fashion. In teaching kids how and when to move we deprive them of the opportunity to think for themselves, to act creatively, to come up with a piece of skill to solve a problem, and maybe in a way that no one could predict.

This is the first point of reflection. Where does skill come from? Can you teach it? If there's one thing that a skill acquisition specialist would agree on it's that skill comes from necessity, and typically it's used to help you with a problem. In this sense it's the problem that creates the skill, not the player. The former Liverpool and England player Peter Beardsley has been described by various people as a genius. His trademarks skills were his quick feet and a feint that would set his opponent off in the wrong direction for long enough to exploit the situation. The type of player that, even if the opponent knew what he was going to do, they still couldn't stop him. Beardsley recalls being invited to a coaching session with a group of kids and the coach asked him to show and explain how he performed his trademark skills. Beardsley recalls that 'embarrassingly' he couldn't do so – essentially he didn't know; he needed the situation, the problem first.

Beardsley was a product of the famous Wallsend Boys Club and had learned his trade playing small-sided 'winner stays on' matches in a football cage. According to Beardsley:

> I used to play five-a-side in what we called the Sweatbox, four or five nights a week in confined surroundings. You learned how to think more quickly on your feet. The tackles would come flying in and if you were kicked it was probably because you'd held the ball too long.[6]

Another example of this 'problem first, solution (skill) second' gave us a famous move that's now taught to kids. Jan Olsson, in an attempt to prevent Johan Cruyff from getting on to his potent left foot, was showing him inside from wide left, but Olsson was left in disbelief as Cruyff feinted to go one way then twisted to go the other. This was no circus act; Cruyff detested showboating. This was a solution to the problem that Olsson had created. In the blink of an eye, Cruyff turned that situation into his favour and with it gave birth to the Cruyff turn. The most remarkable thing about this moment was that this was no training ground move. This was the first time Cruyff had performed this move. Todd Beane, Cruyff's son-in-law and influential coach, explains:

> Johan Cruyff had not practiced that move. He perceived the variables at a given moment, saw the defender poised in assumption, and then decided to make the move [...] The move was born in real time, against a real defender and

the match in flow. It was not a 'move'; it was a solution.[7]

In order to perform the skill in that moment, Cruyff had perceived the movement of the defender and his physical capability, judged where the ball needed to go, and assessed the movement and position of his team-mates on the pitch. Ironically, the solution may have done more harm than good for children around the world who are now taught the Cruyff turn, often without an opponent, simply as a movement and not a solution – we would be better off if we spent less time practising the Cruyff turn and more time creating Olsson problems!

Drills kill skills (and motivation)

Let's look more closely at training ground activities, particularly the previously mentioned training drill, as well as other types of activities. My main area of study over the past two decades has been centred on the development of skill and what types of activities are most suited to creating them. Pertinent to my experiences of football is the question of what role training drills play in the development of skill and, as such, better footballers. I associate a training drill with an activity that's repeated until there's a sense that it has been perfected. You'll know when you see this. They often look complex, involve no opposition player or decision-making, kids often stand at a cone until they're involved in the action, then if the action breaks down it's repeated until it's perfected. In this case we're perfecting the drill, but it does little to develop a skill.

A skill is something that can be applied to the real game, to you and your team's advantage. When it comes to the development of skill, one principle stands out from all others and it's what's called 'the specificity of training principle'. The evidence for the specificity of training effect is so strong that many researchers regard it as not just a general principle of learning but the one that should be the primary consideration when it comes to designing practice activities.

It's a very simple principle and one I always have at the forefront of my mind when designing training sessions for the development of skill: 'if it doesn't 'look like and feel like the real game, don't do it'. For it to meet these conditions, an activity needs to be competitive in nature, the tactical, technical and mental aspects of the game would be present and flowing, and the match would always finish with a result. Much in the same way as the conditions within a video game.

Imagine running a training drill to be better at 'gaming' – what would that look like? Perhaps you would isolate the learner from the challenges of the game and focus on developing the finger movements to operate the controller more effectively. Of course you wouldn't! The brain doesn't know, or care, whether it's learning to play football or a computer game. It just becomes good at whatever it repeatably does. This is why Beardsley couldn't repeat his trademark move, because he hadn't learned it that way, and he had no idea how to perform it when taken out of the context in which he had learned how to do it.

Specificity works like this: if you practise doing Ronaldo 360s with no opposition player around, you'll become better at doing 360s in an open space. If you want to learn how to create space when in a tight position surrounded by opposition players, practise in tight spaces created by opposition players – perhaps a 360 will be needed, perhaps a Cruyff turn or something else.

The problem creates the solution. In the example of the conditions of Beardsley's upbringing in the sweatbox, he became good at performing in tight situations under pressure because he practised in tight spaces while under pressure. Furthermore, as discussed before, these conditions were most probably more difficult than the conditions of a real match situation. Imagine coming from competing in the sweatbox and then playing against a team that had been doing drills all week!

A powerful learning framework for coaches that allows this approach to be applied is called the 'constraints-led approach' (CLA) to coaching. In the CLA the coach designs the learning environment. A CLA is about creating the conditions for learning where skill is learned, not taught. The coach becomes the designer of learning, an architect if you like, who carefully manipulates information to create problems that require skill and ability to develop. In this approach the coach can think of the training field as the 'problem space' – when the players enter the space, they're confronted by problems. Crucially, these problems are 'recognisable' ones that they'll experience in the real match, so they better equip the players with the skills they need in the real environment.

Today, the 'problem space' for most kids is a 4G pitch with little in the way of diversification. It's possible to project into the future the type of player who is going to emerge from these types of environments. Formal training and playing now dominates a child's experience of football, particularly as they get older. This now places a much greater emphasis on the role of the coach and the structure of the practices if we want to develop players with greater skill and creativity.

Solution

Innovation 1 – manipulating constraints

A central way in which the CLA is applied is by manipulating constraints to create highly developmental 'problem spaces'. This is something that may well be familiar to coaches in Systems 1 and 2, but for many it won't be. It's a framework that I believe comes closest to what McLeish was calling for in the 'review' when he called for the recreation of the street but in a modern context. As such, I feel it's a powerful learning tool and one that's being adopted by the most progressive footballing systems around the world.

In my opinion, this is the 'modern context' for learning the game. This is a brief introduction to the concept as it might be a useful addition to current practice, something to experiment with and receive feedback from the players on. To apply it, however, you need to give up a little bit of control. The most developmental learning environments are often the most messy and chaotic ones, where what's 'learned' can't be taught! They don't look organised or for that matter professional, and this has always been a barrier to their implementation. Furthermore, if you want to win your next match or indeed the league in an age-group competition, then you'll get quicker results from running highly organised sessions that drill formations and where everyone knows what their position and role is.

According to Professor Ian Renshaw (a world-leading expert on skill acquisition), traditional approaches lead to 'an incorrect focus on the "mechanics of teaching, such as voice projection, presence, quality of demonstrations, appearance and preparation, and class management", thus failing to address the "learning experience and environment"'.[8]

If you can relinquish winning in the short term for development in the long term, then this is for you. While the environment can seem messy, chaotic and error-strewn, discipline and engagement are seldom a problem. In a well-designed CLA session, boredom isn't a factor. Much like in our video game examples, a well-designed activity will quickly have the learner immersed in the task – the type of immersion you felt just prior to being told you had to go home for your tea!

Another departure from some of our natural tendencies is to try to not jump in and correct when things aren't going as planned. Much like at the skatepark, when trying and failing is the feedback that's needed for further attempts, the environment, as such, is 'safe to fail'. It's expected, not highlighted! The rate and pace of learning, therefore, is out of the control of the coach. The CLA is associated with what's called 'non-linear pedagogy' – it acknowledges that everyone not only learns at different speeds, but that skills and ability have a 'history', and some have been developing them for longer. Not to mention different levels of physical maturity – have I mentioned this already?

The application of a CLA is one where the coach designs a training session by thinking about how constraints can be manipulated to force learning. The three constraints are: task, environment, and the player and/or team. When it comes to 'physical maturity', bio-banding is an example where information has been used to manipulate the player/team for all the positive learning possibilities previously mentioned. This adds a new dimension to the deliberately created 'problem space'.

Crucially, in all CLAs the manipulation contains no information or instruction about what's to be learned, and this opens all sorts of possibilities that you often couldn't have foreseen. It encourages creativity. The same problem can be solved in many ways. Playing two-touch football, where on receiving the ball a player has one touch and then a pass/shot, isn't something I would call a pure CLA because it removes the decision-making aspect from the player. If you manipulate the task, where it's a rule of the game that if you get caught in possession twice in a row you go in the sinbin for two minutes, a player might decide that two touches is a good plan, but they could also solve the problem by getting better at shielding the ball, dribbling or using deception to create space – all potential solutions to the same problem.

When it comes to manipulating the environment, this is typically an approach that changes the size of the pitch or conditions in the environment. Imagine having multiple matches being played on the same pitch but in different directions. What attributes or skills might this force the learner to develop? Trust me, it will look messy and chaotic, unprofessional, but a player will probably want to get their head up and scan their environment, and when they go back to a normal match, trust me, it will feel easier – they might even experience a sense of flow or look a little more gallus in their approach!

Chapter 13

Not the last word

THE STORY of this book began in the 19th century, with the Scots who 'took' the game around the world, who invented the passing game. When I started to piece that story together, I didn't know what I was going to find in this early history. I even questioned whether these sections had a place in the book. Looking for justification, I stumbled upon a paper that UCLA Professor Barbara S. Lawrence wrote in 1984.[1] Lawrence studies organisations to make them better places to work, and suggests that the

> historical perspective refers to understanding a subject in light of its earliest phases and subsequent evolution. This perspective differs from history because its object is to sharpen one's vision of the present, not the past. When historical perspective is overlooked in social research, researchers may draw misleading conclusions.

With these words in mind, I journeyed through the 19th and 20th centuries and found stories about legendary figures who took the game around the world. Stories like these depend on who is telling them. Most countries with a colonial past will have their own football origin stories. I was becoming unconvinced by Lawrence's advice. A romantic notion of our influence on the game wasn't helping to sharpen my vision of the present. However, carry on I did, and thankfully the story started to reveal itself and it became a crucial building block for the rest of the work.

What became clear is that there's little disagreement that the Scots had a profound influence on the way the game would go on to be played. Some of the historical figures mentioned, alongside many more influential Scots, became known collectively as the Scotch Professors. There seems to be no doubt, and little disagreement, that the Scots did indeed invent and popularise the 'passing' game. This crystallised my thinking about why and how this style had emerged, and why others had adopted it.

Mainly it made me contemplate why we're not better at it today. It's not something that's neglected on the training pitches of any elite-level session I've ever seen or lacking in the messaging from high-level coaches during matches. Some may say we instruct players to pass too much. It made me think about the matter of 'our' lack of physicality and how we turned this to our advantage, and yet we don't today.

This then brought me on to a connected line of thinking as we moved into the 20th century. The major theme that emerged, beyond our 'celebrated' history, was that many of our great players had entered professional football at a much later age than is possible today. The system was indeed open longer. Even for those entering at a younger age, it was nowhere near as young as we start selection today. As

I've detailed, this tied in nicely with the 'science' – as it's telling us that we don't know what we're dealing with until maturity kicks in.

For those not shut out of the system, there's a kind of underdog effect, and this can be seen clearly with Andy Robertson and John Collins. The truth is that I could have written a book on Scottish greats who were a little small, were overlooked early and went on to be great players, and for many they became legendary figures. In many ways our identity is linked to this 'apparent' disadvantage; it created the gallus Scot characterisation of a people who wouldn't be taken for granted or belittled – a determination to punch above our weight, to make a better life.

Perhaps my characterisation of today's young player as belonging to the 'achterbankgeneratie' (backseat generation) was a little harsh. But it's hard to ignore that society has changed, and so has football. It's not to suggest that it's not difficult in today's elite system, as children work hard and are disciplined. It's a prerequisite of the privilege of being in the professional system that to some extent this has ripped from them what it was to be a little wild and rough around the edges.

The truth is that the system needs high numbers from all walks of life. More diversity benefits everyone in the talent pool. It creates that much-needed edge. However, we've chosen a path of separation in our quest to get this right. From a talent development perspective, we need to look at how we can deliberately build in desirable difficulties in the progression of a young player. A simple innovation of opening the pathway and by doing so creating more diversity has the potential to add some natural challenge into the system, especially as the characteristics needed to succeed are strongly associated with struggle and overcoming challenges.

Instead, early selection, birth date and maturity status have created a situation where we select what tends to be a homogeneous group of players with little inter-individuality. This simply means that we select similar-looking players with similar attributes and characteristics. This should act as a red flag for those working in System 1. It's an early indication that you've made selection errors. It's not, as some have suggested, that pro-youth coaching is creating robots, but it's closer to say that we're selecting robots to coach.

We're a small country, but we need to make ourselves bigger and utilise the full potential of a talent pool that's vast in numbers. There's simply no shortage of youngsters playing the game, not only that but the organisation of the grassroots game is a key strength that quite simply isn't being tapped into for everyone's benefit, and yet for some there's still an underlying feeling that the elite system caters for too many. Hopefully, the section on talent identification and the random components inherent in a child has shown why we can't rely on our ability to know what a child will be capable of ten years into the future.

The debate on the nature of talent is an important one, and for progress to be made some deeply held beliefs, such as 'you've either got it or you haven't', will need to be consigned to the bin. I've tried to lay the foundations for this argument at the beginning of Section 2. It's natural to use 'subject probability' to make selections because there's currently no other way in which to make these decisions when forced to. And that's the reality of the situation – the system is set up in such way that selection decisions must be made, and made at a young age. This puts unrealistic expectations on all involved.

In the final part of the book, Section 3, I returned to Professor Joe Baker's earlier question, where he asks: 'What would you do for talent selection if you assumed you were terrible at making these decisions instead of assuming you were good?' and I extended it to discuss what I would do in relation to not only selection but also development.

I've argued that due to the random components that skew our judgements we should avoid early selection into the elite academy pathway. There would be no downside to scrapping the early selection concept. Even if this was shown to be wrong, the 'talent' would still rise to the top. We would be no worse off – not better off, but not worse off!

I realise that most people will find my suggestion regarding scrapping the single pathway into the game in favour of a more open 'massive' single system to be too far-fetched. I anticipate a similar reaction to the recommendation that we need multiple pathways and interactions between professional and grassroots clubs. Or the notion of a draft system in the interest of all clubs to be dismissed as pure fantasy. However, I deliberately tried to make some bold recommendations to highlight the size of the job in front of us and the level of innovation that will be needed to turn this situation around. Far-fetched or not, the central premise stands: we need larger numbers, more diversity and policy change when it comes to first-team football if we're to produce a better outcome. A little tweak here and there won't do.

As I write these final remarks, Scotland have not long beaten Georgia 2-0, meaning they have just, for the first time ever, won the first four matches of a qualifying competition. Scotland are now within touching distance of qualifying for the 2024 Euros in Germany. Unfortunately, this success appears to owe more to the quality of our manager than that of our system! Three years on from celebrating the two performance school graduates who made the Euro 2020 squad, the only representative in the win over Georgia was Billy Gilmour. The floodgates of our current approach haven't opened yet. The system in Scotland isn't broken; it was designed this way. However, perhaps it's time to acknowledge that it's a system that needs to be broken to allow a new one to grow back stronger!

Bibliography

Introduction

1 Demirel, D.H. and Yildiran, I., 2013. 'The philosophy of physical education and sport from ancient times to the enlightenment'. *European Journal of Educational Research*, 2(4), pp.191–202.

2 Cobley, S., Baker, J. and Schorer, J., 2020. 'Talent identification and development in sport: an introduction to a field of expanding research and practice'. In *Talent Identification and Development in Sport* (pp. 1–16). Routledge.

3 Rowe, N.F., 2019. 'Sports participation in Scotland: trends and future prospects'. *Observatory for Sport in Scotland:* Kelso, UK.

4 Alley, R.B., Emanuel, K.A. and Zhang, F., 2019. 'Advances in weather prediction'. *Science*, 363(6425), pp.342–344.

5 Farah, L. and Baker, J., 2020. 'Rough draft: The accuracy of athlete selection in North American professional sports'. In *Talent Identification and Development in Sport* (pp. 145–157). Routledge.

6 O'Sullivan, J. 2019. Way of champions. https://wayofchampions. libsyn.com/we-are-all-terrible-at-talent-identification-a-discussion-with-joe-baker

7 The Scottish Youth Football Association registered players and clubs. 2021. www.scottishyouthfa.co.uk/images/newsletters/kickabout/Kickabout-December-2021.pdf

8 Scotland's commissioner for children and young people. 2015. Improving youth football in Scotland. Submission to the Scottish Parliament Public Petitions, Committee on Petition PE1319.

9 The Scottish Football Association. 2023. What is Club academy Scotland? www.scottishfa.co.uk/performance/club-academy-scotland/

10 Celtic F.C. B Team and Academy. 2023. https://en.wikipedia.org/wiki/Celtic_F.C._B_Team_and_Academy#cite_note-47

11 Stirling Albion Junior Academy. 2023. www.stirlingalbionja.co.uk/about

12 McLeish, H., 2020. *Scottish Football: Requiem or Renaissance?* Luath Press Ltd.

13 The Scottish Football Association. 2023. Scottish FA JD Performance Schools www.scottishfa.co.uk/performance/jd-performance-schools/

14 Whyatt, M. 2020. Learning in development. Club culture with reference to youth development vs talent identification. https://podbay.fm/p/learning-in-development/e/1586521850

15 Coerver Coaching. 2023. Player programs. www.coerver.com/products/

16 Coerver coaching. 2023. Learn to play the Benfica way. www.coerverew.
info/benfica

17 English, J. 2018 Anything goes with Andy McLaren. https://jamesenglish.
podbean.com/e/anything-goes-ep19-with-andy-mclaren/

18 Cosgrove, S. 2023 Colt teams' row is a symptom of Scottish football's
avarice. www.thenational.scot/sport/opinion/23505797.colt-teams-row-
symptom-scottish-footballs-avarice/

Chapter 1

1 Lawrence, B.S., 1984. 'Historical perspective: using the past to study the
present, *Academy of Management Review, 9*(2), pp. 307–312.

2 Herman, A., 2001. *How the Scots Invented the Modern World: The True Story
of How Western Europe's Poorest Nation Created Our World & Everything
In It*. Crown.

3 Grant, M. and Robertson, R., 2011. *The Management: Scotland's Great
Football Bosses*. Birlinn.

4 FIFA World Cup records and statistics. 2023. https://en.wikipedia.org/
wiki/FIFA_World_Cup_records_and_statistics#:~:text=As%20of%20
the%202022%20FIFA,nations%20have%20won%20the%20tournament

5 Magoun, F.P., 1938. *History of Football from the Beginnings to 1871* (Vol. 31).
H. Pöppinghaus, oh-g.

6 Vamplew, W., 1982. 'The economics of a sports industry: Scottish
gate-money football, 1890–1914'. *The Economic History Review,
35*(4), pp. 549–567.

7 Magoun, F.P., 1931. 'Scottish popular football, 1424–1815'. *The American
Historical Review, 37*(1), pp.1–13.

8 Phillips, R.J., 1925. *The Story of Scottish Rugby: By RJ Phillips. With 12
Illustrations from Photographs*. TN Foulis.

9 Understanding Glasgow. 2023. Population estimates. www.
understandingglasgow.com/indicators/population/trends/
historic_population_trend#:~:text=Glasgow's%20population%20
1801%2D2021&text=Within%2020%20years%20the%20
population,expansion%20of%20the%20city%20population

10 Collins, T., 2018. *How Football Began: A Global History of How the World's
Football Codes Were Born*. Routledge.

11 Vamplew, W., 2016. 'Scottish football before 1914: an economic analysis of
a gate-money sport'. *Sport in Society, 19*(3), pp. 321–339.

12 Biografias. 2023. Charles William Miller – Introdutor do futebol no
Brasil. https://educacao.uol.com.br/biografias/charles-william-miller.
htm?cmpid=copiaecolahttps://educacao.uol.com.br/biografias/charles-
william-miller.htm

13 Hamilton, A., 1998. *An Entirely Different Game: The British Influence on
Brazilian Football*. Mainstream Publishing Co. (Edinburgh) Ltd.

14 Mason, T., 1995. *Passion of the People? Football in South America*. Verso.

15 Grant, M. and Robertson, R., 2011. *The Management: Scotland's Great
Football Bosses*. Birlinn.

16 Adam, T., 2017. 'The intercultural transfer of football: the contexts of
Germany and Argentina'. *Sport in Society, 20*(10), pp. 1371–1389.

17 Orton, M., 2023. 'The Virile English Game': The Origins of Argentine
Football 1867–1912. In *Football and National Identity in Twentieth-Century
Argentina: La Nuestra* (pp. 17–54). Cham: Springer International Publishing.

18 Orton, M., 2020. *La Nuestra: Football and National Identity in Argentina 1913–1978.*

19 Giulianotti, R., 1999. 'Built by the two Varelas: the rise and fall of football culture and national identity in Uruguay'. *Culture, Sport Society,* 2(3), pp. 134–154.

20 Orton, M., 2017. 'Ants and cicadas: South American football and national identity'. *Midlands Historical Review,* 1, pp. 1–22.

21 Bayce, R., 1991. 'Uruguayan soccer, economy, politics and culture. Never again world champion'.

22 de Rugy, M., 2020. 'Looting and commissioning indigenous maps: James G. Scott in Burma'. *Journal of Historical Geography,* 69, pp. 5–17.

23 Campbell Whittle, I. 2023. Burma-ed and Shanghai-ed. www. scotsfootballworldwide.scot/shanghai-ed

24 Brown, M., 2015. 'British informal empire and the origins of association football in South America'. *Soccer & Society,* 16(2–3), pp. 169–182.

25 Adam, T., 2017. 'The intercultural transfer of football: the contexts of Germany and Argentina'. *Sport in Society,* 20(10), pp. 1371–1389.

26 Dunning, E., 2010. 'Figurational/process-sociological reflections on sport and globalization: some conceptual-theoretical observations with special reference to the 'soccer' form of football'. *European Journal for Sport and Society,* 7(3–4), pp. 183–194.

27 O'Brien, G. ND. The paradoxical structure. http://archive.parliament.scot/ business/committees/enterprise/inquiries/sfi/fic_pt02_O%27Brien.pdf

28 Powley, A., 2015. *Shankly's Village.* eBook Partnership.

29 The Vale of Leven, 2023. The Early Years of Scottish Football. www. valeofleven.org.uk/football02.html

30 Wilson, J., 2018. *Inverting the Pyramid: The History of Football Tactics.* Hachette UK.

31 Kitching, G., 2015, April. 'The origins of football: history, ideology and the making of "The People's Game". *History Workshop Journal,* 79(1), pp. 127–153. Oxford University Press.

32 Scottish Sport History, 2023. Scotland v England in 1872: the first 'official' international. www.scottishsporthistory.com/scotland-v-england-1872.html

33 Alcock, C.W., 1906. *Football: The Association Game.* G. Bell & Sons.

34 Tanner, J. M. 1992. 'Growth as a measure of the nutritional and hygienic status of a population'. *Hormone Research in Paediatrics,* 38(1), pp. 106–115.

35 Kitching, G., 2015, April. 'The origins of football: history, ideology and the making of "The People's Game". *History Workshop Journal,* 79(1), pp. 127–153. Oxford University Press.

36 Macrae, F. 2011. English are now head and shoulders above Scots as growing wealth in the south adds inches to average height. www.dailymail. co.uk/health/article-1374893/English-head-shoulders-Scots-thanks-growing-wealth-south.html

37 World Population Review. 2030. Average Height by Country. https:// worldpopulationreview.com/country-rankings/average-height-by-country

38 The Independent. 2017. Gordon Strachan wants to 'get some big men and women together' to solve Scotland's World Cup woes. https://www. independent.co.uk/sport/football/international/gordon-strachan-scotland-world-cup-2018-genetics-qualifying-a7990151.html

39 Gardasevic, J. and Bjelica, D., 2020. 'Body composition differences between football players of the three top football clubs. *International Journal of Morphology,* 38(1).

40 Kalakoutis, N. 2020. Tactical theory: what football can learn from the famous triangle offence in basketball. https://totalfootballanalysis.com/article/tactical-therory-football-can-learn-famous-triangle-offence-basketball-tactical-analysis-tactics

41 Rincón, J. 2016. Marca. Guardiola's latest group of small players. www.marca.com/en/football/barcelona/2016/10/17/5804c90646163fce3b8b464b.html

42 Carrera, K. Sports Quotes and Facts. Average Height of Premier League Players. https://sqaf.club/average-height-premier-league-player/#:~:text=What%20is%20the%20Average%20Height,Conor%20Gallagher%20of%20Chelsea%20FC

43 Cairney, J., 2004. *A Scottish Football Hall of Fame*. Random House.

44 Strachan, G. 2020. Personal communication.

45 National Records of Scotland, 2023. Webster's Census of 1755 – Scottish Population Statistics. www.nrscotland.gov.uk › census-records

46 Office for National Statistics. 2023. Population estimates for the UK, England, Wales, Scotland and Northern Ireland: mid-2021. www.ons.gov.uk/peoplepopulationandcommunity/populationandmigration/populationestimates/bulletins/annualmidyearpopulationestimates/mid2021

47 Wikipedia. 2023. 1872 Scotland v England football match. https://en.wikipedia.org/wiki/1872_Scotland_v_England_football_match

48 National Records of Scotland. 2023. Births Time Series Data. www.nrscotland.gov.uk/statistics-and-data/statistics/statistics-by-theme/vital-events/births/births-time-series-data

49 The Scottish Public Health Observatory. 2023. Obesity: children's data. www.scotpho.org.uk/clinical-risk-factors/obesity/data/children/

Chapter 2

1 Cairney, J., 2004. *A Scottish Football Hall of Fame*. Random House.

2 Powley, A., 2015. *Shankly's Village*. eBook Partnership.

3 Moffat, A., 2011. *The Scots: A Genetic Journey*. Birlinn.

4 Magnusson, M., 2003. *Scotland: The Story of a Nation*. Grove Press.

5 Craig, G.A., 2002. Great Scots! www.nybooks.com/articles/2002/09/26/great-scots/

6 Braun, H.J., 2013. *Soccer Tactics as Science? On 'Scotch Professors', a Ukrainian Soccer Buddha, and a Catalonian Who Tries to Learn German*. Icon, pp. 216–243.

7 Renton FC. 2023. https://en.wikipedia.org/wiki/Renton_F.C.

8 The Celtic Wiki, 2023. All time A to Z of Celtic players. www.thecelticwiki.com/players/all-time-a-to-z-of-celtic-players/k/kelly-james/

9 The BBC, 1986. *Only A Game – The Story of Scottish Football*.

10 North Lanarkshire Council, 2023. North Lanarkshire's Great Footballers. www.culturenlmuseums.co.uk/story/lanarkshires-great-footballers/

11 Bale, J. and Maguire, J., 2013. *The Global Sports Arena: Athletic Talent Migration in an Interdependent World*. Routledge.

12 Manchester United, 2023. Dennis Law. www.manutd.com/en/players-and-staff/detail/denis-law

13 Bairner, A. 2018. England invented football – but Scots made it the success it has become. https://theconversation.com/england-invented-football-but-scots-made-it-the-success-it-has-become-100691

14 McIlvanney, H. 1997 Busby, Stein & Shankly: The football men. www.youtube.com/watch?v=53TaTp5N4sw

15 FIFA. 2023. The legend and legacy of the Lisbon Lions. www.fifa.com/ fifaplus/en/articles/the-legend-and-legacy-of-the-lisbon-lions

16 Wikipedia, 2023. 1967 European Cup Winners' Cup Final. https:// en.wikipedia.org/wiki/1967_European_Cup_Winners%27_Cup_Final

17 The Scottish Football Museum, 2023. Alex James. www. scottishfootballmuseum.org.uk/exhibitions/hall-of-fame/alex-james/

18 Vital Arsenal. 2022. 'Wee' Alex James. https://arsenal.vitalfootball.co.uk/ wee-alex-james/

19 Harding, J. 2022, Oxford Dictionary of National Biography, James, Alexander Wilson (1901–1953) www.oxforddnb.com/display/10.1093/ ref:odnb/9780198614128.001.0001/odnb-9780198614128-e-34147;jsessioni d=F9A2CD2D379678ED8F2696C800002B96

20 The BBC, 2014. Wembley Wizards 1928. www.bbc.co.uk/scotland/ sportscotland/asportingnation/article/0021/

21 National Football Museum, 2023. Hughie Gallacher. www. nationalfootballmuseum.com/halloffame/hughie-gallacher/

22 Queen of the South, 2023. Legends – Hughie Gallacher. http://qosfc. com/legend-1039

23 Arab Archive, 2022. www.arabarchive.co.uk/matchdetails.php?id=1291

24 UEFA, 2022 Head-to-head. www.uefa.com/uefaeuropaleague/history/ h2h/50079/50080/

25 Dundee Football Club, 2023. 1962/63 European Cup run. https://dundeefc. co.uk/club/history/our-triumphs/196263-european-cup-run/

26 Wikipedia, 2023. 1967 Inter-Cities Fairs Cup Final https://en.wikipedia. org/wiki/1967_Inter-Cities_Fairs_Cup_Final

27 The BBC, 2008. *That Was the Team That Was – Scotland 1974.*

28 The Scottish Football Association, 2023. Scotland at the FIFA World Cup. www.scottishfa.co.uk/scotland/archive/scotland-at-major-tournaments/ scotland-at-the-world-cup/

29 History, 2023. The underachievers: remembering the great Scottish team of the 70s and 80s. www.history.co.uk/article/the-underachievers- remembering-the-great-scottish-team-of-the-70s-and-80s

30 Wikipedia, 2023. List of UEFA club competition-winning managers. https://en.wikipedia.org/wiki/List_of_UEFA_club_competition_ winning_managers

31 FIFA, 2023. 1982 World Cup Spain – Scotland. www.fifa.com/ tournaments/mens/worldcup/1982spain/teams/43967

32 BDFUTBOL, 2023. Rangers 1992/93. www.bdfutbol.com/en/t/ t1992-9310016.html

33 Collins, D. and MacNamara, Á., 2012. 'The rocky road to the top: why talent needs trauma'. *Sports Medicine, 42*, pp. 907–914.

34 Savage, J., Collins, D. and Cruickshank, A., 2017. 'Exploring traumas in the development of talent: what are they, what do they do, and what do they require?' *Journal of Applied Sport Psychology, 29*(1), pp. 101–117.

35 Lareau, A., 2011. *Unequal Childhoods: Class, Race, and Family Life.* Univ of California Press.

36 Wolbert, L.S., de Ruyter, D.J. and Schinkel, A., 2018. 'What attitude should parents have towards their children's future flourishing?' *Theory and Research in Education, 16*(1), pp. 82–97.

37 Binder, J.J. and Findlay, M., 2012. 'The effects of the Bosman ruling on national and club teams in Europe'. *Journal of Sports Economics, 13*(2), pp. 107–129.

38 The Herald, 2005. Unchained: 10 years after Bosman. www.heraldscotland. com/news/12492030.unchained-10-years-after-bosman/
39 SPICe, ND. Briefing for the Public Petitions Committee.
40 UEFA, 2023. Protecting the game: UEFA club licensing. www.uefa.com/ insideuefa/protecting-the-game/club-licensing/documents/
41 UEFA, 2023. UEFA Club Licensing and Financial Sustainability Regulations. https://documents.uefa.com/r/UEFA-Club-Licensing-and-Financial-Sustainability-Regulations-2022-Online

Chapter 3

1 Williams, C. 2019. The Blaes Pitch Project – in memory of the pitches Glasgow youngsters grew up on. www.glasgowlive.co.uk/sport/football/ blaes-pitch-project-memory-pitches-15947441
2 Miller, W., 2013. *The Don: The Willie Miller Story*. Birlinn.
3 Engeser, S. and Rheinberg, F., 2008. 'Flow, performance and moderators of challenge-skill balance'. *Motivation and Emotion, 32*, pp. 158–172.
4 Swann, C., Crust, L., Jackman, P., Vella, S.A., Allen, M.S. and Keegan, R., 2017. 'Psychological states underlying excellent performance in sport: toward an integrated model of flow and clutch states'. *Journal of Applied Sport Psychology, 29*(4), pp. 375–401.
5 Cruyff, J., 2016. *My Turn: The Autobiography*. Macmillan.
6 TED Talks, 2012. Pop an ollie and innovate. www.ted.com/talks/rodney_ mullen_pop_an_ollie_and_innovate
7 Araújo, D., Fonseca, C., Davids, K., Garganta, J., Volossovitch, A., Brandão, R. and Krebs, R., 2010. 'The role of ecological constraints on expertise development'. *Talent Development and Excellence, 2*(2), pp. 165–179
8 Rey, D. 2019. Messi's hometown offers emotional trip to his childhood. https://apnews.com/92b1ef50febe768a8246d356ef098b5f
9 McDonald, H. (2017). 1,000-plus goals and 12 Camanachd cups: Ronaldo of the Glens Ronald Ross is shinty's greatest. www.dailymail.co.uk/ sport/othersports/article-4590444/Ronaldo-Glens-Ronald-Ross-shinty-s-greatest.html
10 Powley, A. and Gillan, R. 2015. *Shankly's Village*. Pitch Publishing.
11 The Scotsman, 2012. Scottish word of the day: Gallus. www.scotsman. com/heritage-and-retro/heritage/scottish-word-day-gallus-2463908
12 Hawley, F.F., 2017. 'The Drag Pit: cockfighting, rationale, and decline'. In *Routledge Handbook on Deviance* (pp. 103–110). Routledge.
13 Lingsur, V., 2020. Ginga – the essence of Brazilian football through the years. www.elartedf.com/ginga-essence-brazilian-football-years/
14 Uehara, L., Button, C., Saunders, J., Araújo, D., Falcous, M. and Davids, K., 2021. 'Malandragem and Ginga: socio-cultural constraints on the development of expertise and skills in Brazilian football'. *International Journal of Sports Science & Coaching, 16*(3), pp. 622–635.
15 Andrews, D.L., Lopes, V.B. and Jackson, S.J., 2015. 'Neymar: sport celebrity and performative cultural politics'. *A Companion to Celebrity*, pp. 421–439.
16 ESPN, 2016. Pele says Brazil need individual ginga to return to their former best. www.espn.com/soccer/brazil/story/2868330/pele-says-brazil-need-individual-%3Ci%3Eginga%3C-i%3E-to-return-to-their-former-best
17 Be Soccer, 2017. Maldini believes 'Italian football needs to start over again'. www.besoccer.com/new/maldini-believes-italian-football-needs-to-start-over-again

18 Tifo Football. 2017. Catenaccio explained. https://www.youtube.com/watch?v=ou44jxozOtc
19 Wilson, J., 2018. *Inverting the Pyramid: The History of Football Tactics*. Hachette UK.
20 Open Goal, 2017. Si Ferry Meets ... James McFadden Episode 1. www.youtube.com/watch?v=5KfhEaLvj_g
21 Arnett, J.J., 1999. 'Adolescent storm and stress, reconsidered'. *American Psychologist*, 54(5), p. 317.
22 Smith, R., 2009. 'Religion, the Scottish work ethic and the spirit of enterprise'. *The International Journal of Entrepreneurship and Innovation*, 10(2), pp. 111–124.
23 Team USA, 2019. www.teamusa.org/USA-Field-Hockey/Features/2019/April/03/Hard-Work-Beats-Talent-When-Talent-Doesnt-Work-Hard
24 Dugan, B., 2007. 'Loss of identity in disaster: how do you say goodbye to home?' *Perspectives in Psychiatric Care*, 43(1), pp. 41–46.
25 n.d. 2020. Andy Roxburgh: headmaster at Carlibar Primary School. https://en-academic.com/dic.nsf/enwiki/310178
26 League Managers Association, 2012. Andy Roxburgh leaves UEFA with a rich legacy. https://web.archive.org/web/20120930021838/http://www.leaguemanagers.com/news/news-7057.html
27 Grant, M. and Robertson, R., 2011. *The Management: Scotland's Great Football Bosses*. Birlinn.
28 Turner, G. and Dart, J., 2013. Football's most successful former teachers. www.theguardian.com/football/2013/aug/14/the-knowledge-football-successful-former-teachers.
29 Camplin, A. 2019. Eddie Jones Aussie PE teacher to English world beater. https://schoolsrugby.com.au/2019/news/eddie-jones-aussie-pe-teacher-to-english-world-beater/
30 James, S., 2014. Belgium's blueprint that gave birth to a golden generation. www.theguardian.com/football/blog/2014/jun/06/belgium-blueprint-gave-birth-golden-generation-world-cup-
31 Kunti, S., 2016. Interview: Belgian Van Winckel spearheads a Saudi football revolution. www.insideworldfootball.com/2016/06/10/interview-belgian-van-winckel-spearheads-saudi-football-revolution/
32 López-Felip, M., 2019. *Collective Behavior in Dissipative Systems: Flocking & Futbol*.
33 Whyatt, M., 2021. Learning in development. https://open.spotify.com/episode/0mOqkDFl7jPwErqFWRk7aU

Chapter 4
1 McLeish, H. 2010. *Review of Scottish Football. Part one: Grassroots, Recreation and Youth Development*. Glasgow: Scottish FA.
2 McLeish, H., 2020. *Scottish Football: Requiem or Renaissance?* Luath Press Ltd.
3 The SFA, 2011. *Scotland United: A 2020 Vision*. Scottish FA.
4 Stone, R., 2022. Tall poppy syndrome is putting an intolerable strain on Scotland's entrepreneurial spirit. www.pressandjournal.co.uk/fp/news/highlands-islands/5637712/golf-coul-links-plan-objections-support/
5 Fife Today, 2016. Fife Elite Academy can be best in Europe. www.fifetoday.co.uk/sport/football/fife-elite-academy-can-be-best-europe-says-new-chairman-henry-mcleish-1192919
6 Bloom, B., (1985). *Developing Talent in Young People*. New York: Ballantine.

7 Scotland's Commissioner for Children and Young People. 2015. Improving Youth Football in Scotland. Submission to the Scottish Parliament Public Petitions, Committee on Petition PE1319.

8 Dweck, C.S., 2006. *Mindset: The New Psychology of Success*. Random House.

9 Ericsson, K.A., 2020. 'Towards a science of the acquisition of expert performance in sports: clarifying the differences between deliberate practice and other types of practice'. *Journal of Sports Sciences, 38*(2), pp. 159–176.

10 Hornig, M., Aust, F. and Güllich, A., 2016. 'Practice and play in the development of German top-level professional football players'. *European Journal of Sport Science, 16*(1), pp. 96–105.

11 Haugaasen, M., Toering, T. and Jordet, G., 2014. 'From childhood to senior professional football: a multi-level approach to elite youth football players' engagement in football-specific activities'. *Psychology of Sport and Exercise, 15*(4), pp. 336–344.

12 Güllich, A., Macnamara, B.N. and Hambrick, D.Z., 2022. 'What makes a champion? Early multidisciplinary practice, not early specialization, predicts world-class performance'. *Perspectives on Psychological Science, 17*(1), pp. 6–29.

13 The Daily Record 2015. Barry Ferguson: www.dailyrecord.co.uk/sport/football/football-news/barry-ferguson-learned-more-five-6823270

Chapter 5

1 The SFA, 2011. *Scotland United: A 2020 Vision*. Scottish FA.

2 The Scottish Football Association. 2023. Scottish FA JD Performance Schools. www.scottishfa.co.uk/performance/jd-performance-schools/

3 McLeish, H., 2020. *Scottish Football: Requiem or Renaissance?* Luath Press Ltd.

4 Gallardo-Gallardo, E., Dries, N. and González-Cruz, T.F., 2013. 'What is the meaning of "talent" in the world of work?' *Human Resource Management Review, 23*(4), pp. 290–300.

5 Wikipedia, 2023. Parable of the talents and minas. https://en.wikipedia.org/wiki/Parable_of_the_talents_or_minas#:~:text=The%20%22Parable%20of%20the%20Talents,the%20third%20received%20only%20one

6 Vinkler, P., 2010. *The Evaluation of Research by Scientometric Indicators*. Oxford, UK: Chandos Publishing.

7 Senior, J. and Gyarmathy, É., 2021. *AI and Developing Human Intelligence: Future Learning and Educational Innovation*. Routledge.

8 Rigney, Daniel., 2010. *The Matthew Effect: How Advantage Begets Further Advantage*. New York: Columbia University Press.

9 Litsky, F., 2004. Doc Counsilman, 83, coach and innovator in swimming. www.nytimes.com/2004/01/05/sports/doc-counsilman-83-coach-and-innovator-in-swimming.html

10 Gruber, H., Jansen, P., Marienhagen, J. and Altenmueller, E. (2010). 'Adaptations during the acquisition of expertise'. *Talent Development & Excellence of Expertise, 2*(1), pp. 3–15.

11 Nesti, M. and Sulley, C., 2014. *Youth Development in Football: Lessons from the World's Best Academies*. Routledge.

Chapter 6

1 Williams, G. and MacNamara, Á., 2020. '"I didn't make it, but...": deselected athletes' experiences of the talent development pathway'. *Frontiers in Sports and Active Living*, p. 24.

2 Schorer, J., Rienhoff, R., Fischer, L. and Baker, J., 2017. 'Long-term prognostic validity of talent selections: comparing national and regional coaches, laypersons and novices'. *Frontiers in Psychology, 8*, p. 1146.

3 Dugdale, J.H., Sanders, D., Myers, T., Williams, A.M. and Hunter, A.M., 2021. 'Progression from youth to professional soccer: a longitudinal study of successful and unsuccessful academy graduates'. *Scandinavian Journal of Medicine & Science in Sports*, *31*, pp. 73–84.

4 Tucker, R. 2019. The Real Science of Sport Podcast. How to make a champion (Pt1). https://shows.acast.com/realscienceofsport/episodes/howtomakeachampion

5 Clear, J., 2019. *Atomic habits: an easy and proven way to build good habits and break bad ones: tiny changes, remarkable results. (No Title)*. Random House

6 The Rangers Rabble podcast. 2022. Interview with Craig Mulholland. www.youtube.com/watch?v=ySixieff5MU

7 The Heart of Midlothian Football Club (2023). The Football Academy. www.heartsfc.co.uk/squads/academy/overview

8 Motherwell Football Club. 2023. Recruitment and scouting. www.motherwellfc.co.uk/club/academy/recruitment-scouting/

9 The Scottish FA. (2017). Project Brave presentations kick-off. www.scottishfa.co.uk/news/project-brave-presentations-kick-off/

10 Crann, J., 2022. Sheffield Wednesday boss on 'hotbed of talent' in Scotland amid links to Motherwell starlet. www.thestar.co.uk/sport/football/sheffield-wednesday/sheffield-wednesday-boss-on-hotbed-of-talent-in-scotland-amid-links-to-motherwell-starlet-3872017

11 Dinnie, B. 2014. *The Scout: The Bobby Dinnie Story*. Shn

12 Dalglish, K., 2013. *Kenny Dalglish: My Life*. Trinity Mirror Sport Media.

13 Glasgow Times, 2007. Just an ordinary wee guy. www.glasgowtimes.co.uk/news/12784371.im-just-an-ordinary-wee-guy-says-the-man-who-discovered-king-kenny/

14 McNeil, R. nd. Jim Baxter remembered as we salute Rangers and Scotland legend. www.heraldscotland.com/sport/23315843.jim-baxter-remembered-salute-rangers-scotland-legend/

15 Hart, R., 2016. Academy wants to find the next Broony. www.centralfifetimes.com/sport/14794041.academy-wants-to-find-the-next-broony/

16 Hutchison Vale Community Sports Club, 2013. A thumbnail sketch of Hutchie from 1940–to present day. www.hutchisonvale.com/the-club/our-history/

17 Scotland's Commissioner for Children and Young People. 2015. Improving Youth Football in Scotland. Submission to the Scottish Parliament Public Petitions, Committee on Petition PE1319.

18 Hunter, G., 2019. The Big Interview with Graham Hunter, John Collins. https://grahamhunter.tv/classic-big-interview-john-collins/

19 Cumbernauld United, 2023. The Club. https://cumbernauldunited.co.uk/theclub/

20 Lewis, M., 2016. The undoing project: A friendship that changed the world. Penguin UK

21 Ankersen, R., 2012. *The Gold Mine Effect: Crack the Secrets of High Performance*. Icon Books Ltd.

22 Pearce, J., 2017. The Andy Robertson story – from answering phones at Hampden Park to his Liverpool dream. www.liverpoolecho.co.uk/sport/football/football-news/liverpool-andy-robertson-jurgen-klopp-13397200

Chapter 7

1 Pedersen, A.V., Aune, T.K., Dalen, T. and Lorås, H., 2022. 'Variations in the relative age effect with age and sex, and over time – Elite-level data from international soccer world cups'. *Plos one*, *17*(4), p.e0264813.

2 Dugdale, J.H., McRobert, A.P. and Unnithan, V.B., 2021. '"He's just a wee laddie": The relative age effect in male Scottish soccer'. *Frontiers in Psychology*, p. 103.

3 Barcelona FCB, 2023. Soccer – Cadet B – Squad 2022–23. www. fcbarcelona.es/es/futbol/formativo-masculino/cadete-b/jugadores

4 Doyle, J.R. and Bottomley, P.A., 2018. 'Relative age effect in elite soccer: more early-born players, but no better valued, and no paragon clubs or countries'. *PloS one*, *13*(2), p.e0192209.

5 De Hong, M., 2020 The curious tale of the football international nobody ever heard of (because he was born in the wrong month). https://thecorrespondent.com/406/the-curious-tale-of-the-football-international-nobody-ever-heard-of-because-he-was-born-in-the-wrong-month/53750016012-f852949c

6 Whyatt, M. O'Sullivan, M. & Thomas, B., 2020. Club culture with reference to youth development vs talent identification. https://podcasts. apple.com/se/podcast/learning-in-development/id1507378548?l=en &i=1000471395882

7 Smith, E. 2020. 'I wasn't good enough at all' – Van Dijk reveals he was nearly axed by his first academy. www.goal.com/en-gb/news/i-wasnt-good-enough-at-all-van-dijk-nearly-axed-first/19zj037yvqgz91nr5gqfvd9pyv

8 Kuper, S., 2019. Virgil van Dijk is the best player in the Premier League: how the Dutch defender became Liverpool's leader. https://africa.espn. com/football/club/liverpool/364/blog/post/3824468/virgil-van-dijk-is-the-best-player-in-the-premier-league-how-the-dutch-defender-became-liverpools-leader

9 Celtic FC, 2021. The Celtic View Podcast 2021 E50 With Chris McCart. www.youtube.com/watch?v=sgyfKfCFHw0

10 Hill, M., John, T., McGee, D. and Cumming, S.P., 2023. '"He's got growth": coaches understanding and management of the growth spurt in male academy football'. *International Journal of Sports Science & Coaching*, *18*(1), pp. 24–37.

11 Sweeney, L., Cumming, S.P., MacNamara, Á. and Horan, D., 2022. 'A tale of two selection biases: the independent effects of relative age and biological maturity on player selection in the Football Association of Ireland's national talent pathway'. *International Journal of Sports Science & Coaching*.

12 Ostojic, S.M., Castagna, C., Calleja-González, J., Jukic, I., Idrizovic, K. and Stojanovic, M., 2014. 'The biological age of 14-year-old boys and success in adult soccer: do early maturers predominate in the top-level game?' *Research in Sports Medicine*, *22*(4), pp. 398–407.

13 Tucker, R., 2019. The Real Science of Sport Podcast. How to make a champion (Pt1). https://shows.acast.com/realscienceofsport/episodes/howtomakeachampion

14 Tucker, R. 2019. The Real Science of Sport Podcast. How to make a champion (Pt1). https://shows.acast.com/realscienceofsport/episodes/howtomakeachampion

Chapter 8

1 Hibernian Football Club, 2023. A pathway for the wee Hibees. www. hibernianfc.co.uk/article/a-pathway-for-the-wee-hibees

2 Binder, J. J., and Findlay, M., 2012. 'The effects of the Bosman Ruling on national and club teams in Europe'. *Journal of Sports Economics*, *13*(2), pp. 107–129.

3 Sky Sports, 2022. Premier League had only 13 foreign players in 1992. www.skysports.com/football/news/11095/12671228/premier-league-had-only-13-foreign-players-in-1992-craig-forrest-and-michel-vonk-explain-what-it-was-like-for-them

4 McLeish, H., 2020. *Scottish Football: Requiem Or Renaissance?* Luath Press Ltd.

5 Nesti, M. and Sulley, C., 2014. *Youth Development in Football: Lessons from the World's Best Academies.* Routledge.

6 Owen, G. 2013. Greg Dyke aims for an England World Cup win at Qatar 2022. www.theguardian.com/football/2013/sep/04/greg-dyke-england-world-cup-qatar-2022

7 The FA, 2015. FA chairman's update on England commission. www.thefa.com/news/2015/mar/23/greg-dyke-england-commission-homegrown-players-work-permits-march-2015

8 Wilson, J., 2022. Remember Greg Dyke's clock? It still exists – and is about to hit zero. www.telegraph.co.uk/world-cup/2022/11/20/remember-greg-dykes-clock-still-exists-hit-zero/

9 Coyle, A., 2021. Deal agreed to help SPFL clubs continue to sign overseas players. https://news.stv.tv/sport/deal-agreed-to-help-spfl-clubs-continue-to-sign-overseas-players

10 Lowe, S., 2021. Real Sociedad are in LaLiga's title race and they're doing it by developing talent from within. www.espn.com/soccer/real-sociedad/story/4513541/real-sociedad-are-in-laligas-title-race-and-theyre-doing-it-by-developing-talent-from-within

11 Lowe, S., 2021. Goals, class, a red Ferrari: Aldridge, Richardson and Atkinson at la Real. www.theguardian.com/football/blog/2021/feb/25/aldridge-richardson-and-atkinson-at-real-sociedad-goals-class-red-ferrari

12 Clapham, A., 2019. Inside Real Sociedad, a football club shaped by its academy. www.theguardian.com/football/2019/dec/24/real-sociedad-football-club-academy-la-liga

13 Castillo, J., 2008. 'The other Basque subversives: Athletic de Bilbao vs. the new age of soccer'. *Sport in Society*, *11*(6), pp. 711–721.

14 Clapham, A., 2018. How does Athletic Bilbao's academy manage to produce 85% of their team? www.theguardian.com/football/2018/oct/30/athletic-bilbao-players-la-liga

15 Rojo, L., n.d. Barcelona's new model leaving La Masia behind. www.marca.com/en/football/barcelona/2016/09/01/57c843d022601dea758b45fd.html

16 Rees, L. n.d. An integrated approach to developing sporting excellence. www.aspetar.com/journal/upload/PDF/201867194815.pdf

17 Rueben J., 2022. Debt-ridden Barcelona was king of the 2022 transfer window, but at what cost? www.thehindu.com/sport/football/debt-ridden-barcelona-was-king-of-the-2022-transfer-window-but-at-what-cost/article65848832.ece#:~:text=The%20market%20crisis&text=It%20spent%20the%20money%20on,above%20%E2%82%AC140%20million%20each

Chapter 9

1 PE1319: Improving Youth Football in Scotland https://digitalpublications.parliament.scot/Committees/Report/PPC/2020/6/22/PE1319--Improving-youth-football-in-Scotland

2 Hall, R., Foss, K.B., Hewett, T.E. and Myer, G.D., 2015. Sport specialization's association with an increased risk of developing anterior knee pain in adolescent female athletes. Journal of sport rehabilitation, 24(1), pp.31-35.

3 Mostafavifar, A.M., Best, T.M. and Myer, G.D., 2013. Early sport specialisation, does it lead to long-term problems?. British journal of sports medicine, 47(17), pp.1060-1061.
4 Herron, L. 2015. Jim McInally blasts Scottish youth system by insisting rejection drove players to brink. www.express.co.uk/sport/football/619099/ Jim-McInally-blasts-Scottish-youth-system-by-insisting-rejection-drove-players-to-brink
5 McWhorter, J., 2011. Path Dependency. www.edge.org/response-detail/10852
6 Bergek, A. and Onufrey, K., 2014. 'Is one path enough? Multiple paths and path interaction as an extension of path dependency theory'. *Industrial and Corporate Change*, *23*(5), pp. 1261–1297.
7 Djelic, M.L. and Quack, S., 2007. 'Overcoming path dependency: path generation in open systems'. *Theory and Society*, *36*, pp. 161–186.

Chapter 10
1 Overvik, J., 2020. Erling Braut Haalands, unique upbringing researched: this is how he became good. www.vg.no/sport/fotball/i/50znPX/erling-braut-haalands-unike-oppvekst-forsket-paa-slik-ble-han-god
2 O Sullivan, M., 2020. Erling Haaland – As many as possible, as long as possible, as good as possible. https://footblogball.wordpress.com/2020/03/08/erling-braut-halland-as-many-as-possible-as-long-as-possible-as-good-as-possible/
3 Andrew, R., 2022. The LTAD Network podcast. Dr Sean Cumming. https://podcasters.spotify.com/pod/show/ltadnetworkpodcast/episodes/Dr-Sean-Cumming-Bath-University-An-idiots-guide-to-Growth--Maturation-and-Biobanding-e9bs5f
4 Walker, J., 2021. Scots Abroad. Lewis Morgan. https://open.spotify.com/episode/3JtWc73stxIT1BueYUtJih

Chapter 11
1 Honigstein, R., 2015. *Das Reboot: How German Soccer Reinvented Itself and Conquered the World*. Bold Type Books.
2 Poli, R., Ravenel, L., and Besson, R., 2022. Financial analysis of big-5 league clubs' transfers. www.football-observatory.com/IMG/sites/mr/mr77/en/
3 Footballscience.net. 2023. Top clubs for U20 players' employment. www.footballscience.net/2023/05/12/top-clubs-for-u20-players-employment/
4 Erkkilä, A., 2019. 'The factors behind successful immigrant athletes'.
5 Britannica. 2023. Immigration of France. www.britannica.com/place/France/Immigration
6 Auclair, P., 2012, *Thierry Henry: Lonely at the Top*. Paperback
7 Petrilla, C., Matteson, D., Silva, D., Mannion, S. and Huggins, S., 2021. 'Cultivating positive youth development through Latin American street soccer programming'. *Journal of Child and Youth Care Work*, *27*.
8 Marques, R., Schubring, A., Barker-Ruchti, N., Nunomura, M. and Menezes, R., 2021. 'From soccer to futsal: Brazilian elite level men players' career pathways'. *Soccer & Society*, *22*(5), pp. 486–501.
9 Uehara, L., Davids, K., Pepping, G., Gray, R. and Button, C., 2022. 'The role of family and football academy in developing'. *International Sports Studies*, *44*(2), pp. 6–21.
10 Teixeira, A., Valente-dos-Santos, J., Coelho-e-Silva, M., Malina, R., Fernandes-da-Silva, J., do Nascimento Salvador, P., De Lucas, R., Wayhs,

M. and Guglielmo, L. 2015. 'Skeletal maturation and aerobic performance in young soccer players from professional academies'. *International Journal of Sports Medicine*, *36*(13), pp. 1069–1075.

11 Homewood, B. 2014. Germany debacle the culmination of long Brazil decline. www.reuters.com/article/uk-soccer-world-bra-analysis-idUKKBN0FE2CK20140709

12 Abd Karim, Z., Ramalu, R., Mohamad, S., Miranda, E., Abd Malek, N. and Adnan, M., 2022. *The Brazilian Football Player's Supernatural Talent Development: A Qualitative Study.*

13 N.d. www.ucl.ac.uk/atlas/dutch/sport.html#:~:text=Football,has%20produced%20many%20famous%20players

14 The Dutch model of developing young footballers: let them sink or swimwww.theguardian.com/football/2019/aug/20/eredivisie-clubs-ajax-psv-az-utrecht-teams-dutch

15 Personal communication with Craig Brown.

16 Jackson, J., 2015. Jamie Vardy, the Stocksbridge Park Steels striker who went on to England. www.theguardian.com/football/2015/jun/06/leicester-jamie-vardy-non-league-england

17 Scotland Census., 2021. Ethnicity. www.scotlandscensus.gov.uk/census-results/at-a-glance/ethnicity/

18 Randhawa, K., 2012. 'Marrying Passion with Professionalism: Examining the Future of British Asian Football', in Burdsey, D. (ed.), *Race, Ethnicity and Football* (pp. 240–253). Routledge.

19 Coyle, D., 2009. *The Talent Code: Greatness Isn't Born, it's Grown. Here's How.* Bantam.

20 Nazir, T., James, K., Abdurahman, M. and Al-Khazraji, H., 2022. 'Pakistani support for Glasgow's Old Firm football clubs'. *Soccer & Society*, *23*(7), pp. 784–804.

21 Chelsea FC., 2023. Chelsea Asian Star. www.chelseafc.com/en/chelsea-foundation-asian-star

Chapter 12

1 Ford, P., Carling, C., Garces, M., Marques, M., Miguel, C., Farrant, A., Stenling, A., Moreno, J., Le Gall, F., Holmström, S. and Salmela, J. 2012. 'The developmental activities of elite soccer players aged under-16 years from Brazil, England, France, Ghana, Mexico, Portugal and Sweden'. *Journal of Sports Sciences*, *30*(15), pp. 1653–1663.

2 Hunter, G., 2015. The Big Interview with Graham Hunter. Graeme Souness: the winning gene. https://podcasts.apple.com/ca/podcast/graeme-souness-the-winning-gene/id988360681?i=1000356223325

3 Kroeten, T. 2019. The world's finest youth academy is not the best developmental system. www.joyofthepeople.org/post/2019/05/01/the-worlds-finest-youth-academy-is-not-the-best-developmental-system

4 Wikipedia. 2023 Mateo Kovačić https://en.wikipedia.org/wiki/Mateo_Kova%C4%8Di%C4%87

5 Howard, J., Bureau, J., Guay, F., Chong, J. and Ryan, R., 2021. 'Student motivation and associated outcomes: a meta-analysis from self-determination theory'. *Perspectives on Psychological Science*, *16*(6), pp. 1300–1323.

6 Corrigan, MJ., 2015. The unorthodox genius of Peter Beardsley. https://thesefootballtimes.co/2015/04/09/the-unorthodox-genius-of-peter-beardsley/

7 Beane, T. TOVO Institute. I wish Wiel Coerver got it right. 2017. https://www.tovoinstitute.com/2017-10-27-i-wish-wiel-coerver-got-it-right/
8 Renshaw, I., Araújo, D., Button, C., Chow, J., Davids, K. and Moy, B., 2016. 'Why the constraints-led approach is not teaching games for understanding: a clarification'. *Physical Education and Sport Pedagogy*, *21*(5), pp. 459–480.

Chapter 13
1 Lawrence, B. 1984. 'Historical perspective: using the past to study the present'. *Academy of Management Review*, *9*(2), pp. 307–312.